CHAM

A DICTIONARY OF
CROSSWORD ABBREVIATIONS

Michael Kindred and Derrick Knight

CHAMBERS

CHAMBERS

An imprint of Chambers Harrap Publishers Ltd
7 Hopetoun Crescent
Edinburgh
EH7 4AY

www.chambers.co.uk

First published by Chambers Harrap Publishers Ltd 2005

ISBN 0550 10173 X

Editorial Consultants: Derek Arthur and Ross Beresford

Chambers Editor: Hazel Norris

Editorial Assistance: Camilla Rockwood

Data Management: Patrick Gaherty

Prepress Controllers: Vienna Leigh and Isla MacLean

Prepress Manager: Sharon McTeir

Publishing Manager: Patrick White

Designed and typeset by Chambers Harrap Publishers Ltd, Edinburgh
Printed by Cox & Wyman Ltd, Reading, Berkshire

CONTENTS

Acknowledgements

We are indebted to Hazel Norris of Chambers for her painstaking and thorough editing. She encouraged us with humour, accuracy and patience. Further editing was carried out by Ross Beresford, assisted by Derek Arthur. It is an honour to have their input.

Important contributions were made by Georgie Johnson, who vetted our drafts and made useful suggestions for additions and amendments, and by Margaret Hopkinson, who fed Derrick suggestions from *The Daily Telegraph*.

Finally our thanks are due to those anonymous setters who struggle on a daily basis to find new ways of clueing words.

About the Authors

As a professional active listener – a therapeutic counsellor – it was natural that Derrick Knight should be drawn to *The Listener* crossword. This led, 15 years ago, to an active sideline in setting cryptic crosswords under the pseudonym Mordred (an evil Knight). He now sets for *The Listener* crossword, *The Independent*'s Saturday Magazine, *The Sunday Telegraph* EV series, *The Magpie* crossword magazine and *Crossword* (the monthly magazine of the Crossword Club).

Michael Kindred has been an inventor of board and card games and an author and publisher of educational books and training materials since the 1960s. He sets for *The Listener* crossword as Emkay.

Michael Kindred and Derrick Knight are the authors of *Cryptic Crosswords and How to Solve Them*, a guide to help fledgling crossword solvers develop their skills using a series of graded puzzles, which is also available from Chambers.

INTRODUCTION

Abbreviations are a key part of cryptic crossword solving. Setters use abbreviations as 'building blocks' from which solvers can piece together the different parts of a solution. For example, take the clue:

'Argue city is in Switzerland (5)'

'Argue' is the definition of the answer, which means that 'city is in Switzerland' forms the 'wordplay' or cryptic element of the clue. Here there are no fewer than three components requiring abbreviation:

- an abbreviation of an example of a 'city' = LA (for Los Angeles)
- an abbreviation of the word 'is' = S
- an abbreviation of the country name 'Switzerland' = CH

Placing LA + S inside 'CH' leaves us with CLASH, and the clue is solved.

You might think that there are enough dictionaries of abbreviations already, and these abbreviations would have been easy enough to find. However, what makes *XWD* unique is that entries are given in a form useful to crossword solvers, with an eye to how they would be likely to appear in clues.

In any standard dictionary, or one of abbreviations, LA would be found under L, and CH under C. Solvers would have no way of knowing that the city required was LA, nor that the abbreviation for Switzerland did not begin with S. This renders conventional tools of the cryptic crossword trade useless. In *XWD*, they would simply need to look under 'city' and 'Switzerland' respectively to find the answers they need.

This is especially useful when the abbreviations used seem to bear no relation to their full forms. A favourite among cryptic crossword setters is the abbreviation SP, which is clued as 'without issue'. To find this abbreviation in a normal dictionary you would need to know that the Latin version is 'sine prole', hence the abbreviation SP. Solvers lacking this key piece of information might think that the letters WI were required, and spend many fruitless hours pondering what the answer could be. Using *XWD*, they can look up 'without issue' and immediately find that SP are the letters sought.

Organization

XWD is divided into two parts. Part One lists full words and phrases in alphabetical order with the possible abbreviations alongside. Part Two reverses this process and lists abbreviations in alphabetical order with their associated full forms.

All abbreviations are shown in the form in which solvers are expected to enter them in the grid. They are all in upper case and, where there would normally be a division between two words in an abbreviation, the space has been omitted. ET AL, for example, thus becomes ETAL.

An exception is the digit 1, which has been kept as a number in the text for clarity, but which would normally be entered in the crossword grid as the letter I. For example, the abbreviation M1 for 'motorway' would be entered as MI.

Introduction

As usual in crossword entries, accents have been ignored. Similarly, punctuation has been omitted: there are no apostrophes, hyphens, forward slashes, full stops and the like. A/C, for example, is listed simply as AC.

Inclusion

XWD includes thousands of abbreviations which might form part of the solutions to cryptic crossword clues, arranged into more than 10,000 entries. It is not an exhaustive list; only those abbreviations likely to be used in cryptic crosswords have been included. For example, the abbreviation SPQR, for 'the Senate and the People of Rome', would be hard for a setter to include as part of a word, and its full form is too long to fit into the space normally acceptable for a clue. It has therefore been excluded.

In deciding what to include in *XWD*, the net has been cast wide. In addition to common abbreviations, you will find useful short forms, contractions, symbols, the NATO phonetic alphabet, International Vehicle Registration codes, state codes and acronyms. Shortened forms of first names have been included in some cases. There are also entries such as that for 'note', which lists A, B, C, etc, which are not strictly abbreviations but which are found so often in crosswords that their inclusion was thought to be helpful. Terms have been drawn primarily from *The Chambers Dictionary*, but have been augmented with abbreviations from other sources, including numerous actual examples from several national newspapers.

As with all crossword devices, abbreviations acceptable to some setters, solvers and newspaper crossword editors will be frowned upon by others. T for 'shirt' or for 'model' is an example of this. A T-shirt is a type of shirt and so should be clued as 'type of shirt'. You will often, however, find it clued simply as 'shirt'. This is an instance of definition by example, and it is unacceptable to some people. However, as you are likely to find these kinds of terms in crosswords, they have been included in this book.

Solvers used to tackling crosswords from newspapers and magazines should also remember that different publications have their own individual lists of what are considered to be acceptable abbreviations. Some setters and publications exclude little-known abbreviations; others take delight in finding ways to use obscure terms. The coverage of *XWD* is intended to be as broad as possible, and has been drawn from a variety of sources so as not to be constrained by the conventions of only a certain newspaper or, indeed, dictionary.

Plurals

Where an abbreviation stands for both singular and plural full forms this has been indicated with an 's' in brackets at the end of the full form. Where the plural differs from simply adding an 's' there is a separate entry.

Where a full form adds an 's' to make the plural, and the abbreviation does the same, only the singular form of each is shown.

Appendices

Where a large number of possible abbreviations exist for a particular entry, such as 'state' which usually indicates a US state, solvers are referred to the Appendices. A list of the information which can be found in the Appendices is given in the contents list at the start of the book.

Explanations of the Abbreviations

Sometimes it can be hard to understand why a particular word is abbreviated in a certain way. Why, for example, is R an abbreviation for 'take'? Space does not allow for explanation of reasons in *XWD*, and solvers are referred instead to *The Chambers Dictionary* if they wish to know more of the background to a particular term. Here they will find that 'take' is abbreviated to R because 'recipe' was the Latin word for 'take'.

Old Terms

Older abbreviations, such as BR for 'British Rail', or D for 'penny', whilst no longer generally in use, are still found in dictionaries, and may be used in crossword clues. They are therefore included in *XWD*. When used in clues there will generally be something to indicate that they are no longer current: BR might be clued as 'former railway', whilst D may be 'old penny'.

THE USE OF ABBREVIATIONS
IN CRYPTIC CROSSWORDS

How to Recognize When an Abbreviation is Needed

Abbreviations, like anagrams, are a key part of many cryptic crossword clues. But while the use of an anagram in a cryptic clue will usually be indicated to the solver by the use of words such as 'confused' or 'upset', abbreviations are not so clearly signposted. The difficult task for the solver is to decide whether the wordplay element of the clue contains a word or phrase that has to be abbreviated to form part of the solution.

There are certain words, however, that very often lead to abbreviations. 'State' often requires the abbreviation of a US state. The name of any country, especially when preceded by 'in', as in the 'clash' clue explained in the Introduction, will often require an abbreviation of that country. 'Boy' or 'girl' may require a diminutive of a first name. 'City', again as used in the 'clash' clue, usually represents LA, NY or EC. 'Old city' is often UR, which is, of course, not an abbreviation. It could also be OLA or ONY.

'Direction', 'key', 'partner', 'opponent' and the like are also fairly common abbreviation indicators. But there are many others that solvers must learn as part of their crossword armoury, and working out what these are is part of the fun of learning to solve cryptic crosswords.

Single Abbreviation Wordplay

Clues in cryptic crosswords usually contain a definition of the answer together with elements that make up that word or words. These elements are known as 'wordplay', and this is where the parts of the clue which lead to abbreviations will be found.

Setters are often content to make use of one abbreviation to help them clue the answer. Try, for example:

'Hidden city shelter (6)'

As in the 'clash' clue discussed in the Introduction, here LA has been used for 'city'. This time it is followed by a normal substitute for 'shelter': 'tent', to give 'latent', a synonym for 'hidden'.

Most cryptic crosswords will contain clues such as this in which an abbreviation is paired with an unabbreviated word.

Multiple Abbreviation Wordplay

Sometimes more than one abbreviation is used as a block to build up the elements of the solution. In the 'clash' example, there are three abbreviations used in the wordplay to make up a single-word solution. As explained in the Introduction, the wordplay element is 'city is in Switzerland'. Solvers are required to place LA for 'city' and S for 'is' inside CH for 'Switzerland'.

A harder clue of the same construction might be:

'Died without issue in hot Italian sanatorium (8)'

Here, our old friend 'without issue', discussed in the Introduction, reappears with a twist. This time the abbreviation required is 'Died without issue', which is OSP. Solvers are required to place OSP inside H (hot) and ITAL (Italian). 'Sanatorium' can now be recognized as the definition part of the clue, leading of course to 'hospital'.

Another example:

'Settle firm position held by state (7)'

This is in a similar vein to the last clue, with a slightly different construction. Here 'settle' is the definition element of the clue. In the wordplay, CO is used for 'firm', POS for 'position' and ME for 'state'. The difference is that POS is 'held by', or placed inside, ME, with CO before it, leading to the answer: 'compose'.

An even more complex clue which demands more of the solver might be:

'British Moonies need no money in dull provincial place (7)'

Here both B for 'British' and M for 'money' come into play. On this occasion there is 'no money', so M must be removed from B + Moonies to provide the solution: 'boonies'.

In clues such as this an abbreviation has to be removed, whereas in the first examples one abbreviation has to be placed inside another. Otherwise, however, the separate elements of the clue usually follow each other in order. For example:

'Hateful overdraft debts (6)'

Here there are two consecutive abbreviations: OD for 'overdraft', plus IOUS for 'debts'.

More devious would be:

'Having a dislike of Cambridge I would finally leave (4,5)'

CANTAB is the abbreviation for 'of Cambridge', I is simply 'I', D is the abbreviation for 'would' and E is the last letter of 'leave' (its use indicated by 'finally'). This becomes CANT ABIDE, the apostrophe having been ignored, as is usual in grid entries.

A simpler variation is:

'Bird of prey originally flying about Lake Constance (6)'

In this case the first letter of 'flying' (indicated by 'originally') is employed before A as an abbreviation for 'about', L for 'Lake', and CON for 'Constance', giving us 'falcon' as the bird of prey in the solution.

Linking Words

There are a number of words that it is acceptable to include in a clue which are not essential to the wordplay, but which help to make a sensible sentence. These include 'and', 'the', 'to', 'of', 'is', 'in', 'with', 'or' and similar terms. However, solvers should never assume these are merely linking words. In the 'clash' clue in the Introduction,

The Use of Abbreviations in Cryptic Crosswords

this assumption would have hindered solving, because 'is' needed to be abbreviated and 'in' was an essential ingredient, directing solvers to how to put the abbreviation building blocks together. It is always a golden rule when solving to note each word very carefully – you never know when an apparently straightforward linking word might actually have a hidden meaning in the clue.

Acronyms

'Double definition' clues are formed from two or more words which each have similar meanings to the answer. Acronyms and other abbreviations lend themselves beautifully to this.

'Short memory (4)'

produces DRAM. Another:

'Offers an Internet service (4)'

leads us to BIDS.

Foreign and Archaic Terms

When setters use an English word in the wordplay of a clue and they require a foreign equivalent of it to be incorporated in the solution they should indicate this in the wordplay. For example, CIE is an abbreviation of the French word 'compagnie', and so should always be clued as 'French company' rather than just 'company'.

Similarly, archaic indicators should apply to abbreviations of words no longer in general use, such as BR and D, as mentioned in the Introduction. 'Old penny' could, of course be an indicator for OP as well as D.

PART ONE
FULL FORM ⇨ ABBREVIATION

abbess; abbey; abbot	ABB	accident	CVA; RTA
abbreviated; abbreviation	ABBR; ABBREV	Accident Compensation Corporation	ACC
abdicated	ABD	accident preventers	ROSPA
abdominal muscle	AB	accompanied	ACC
Aberdeen	ABER	accompanist	COMP
ablative	ABL	according	ACC
about	A; APPROX; C; CA; CIR; CIRC; RE	according to art	SA
		according to nature	SN
above	SUP	according to rule	SECREG
above mean sea level	AMSL	to value	ADVAL
Abraham	ABE; BRAM	account	AC; ACC; ACCT
abridged	ABD; ABR	account current	AC
abridgement	ABR	account executive	AE
absence	ABS	accountant	ACA; ACC; ACCA; CA; CPA; FCA; FCCA; FCMA
absent	A; ABS; AWOL; MIA		
absolute	A; ABS; ABSOL	accountants	ACCA; ACMA; ICA
absolutely	ABS; ABSOL		
absorbent	ABS	Accounting Standards Board	ASB
abstainers	AA; TT		
abstaining; abstemious	TT	accusative	ACC; ACCUS
abstract	ABS; ABSTR	AC/DC	BI
academic	BA; MA; PROF; see also Appendix: Degrees	ace	A; I
		achievement quotient	AQ
academic institution	see university and Appendix: Colleges	acid	AHA; ALA; CLA; DNA; EDTA; EFA; EPA; GLA; IAA; LSD; PABA; PAS; PNA; RNA
academician	A; ARA; RA		
academy	A; BA; NAS; RA; RADA; RAM; RCA; RSA	acid test; acidity	PH
		ack-ack	AA
		acre	A; AC
accelerando	ACCEL	acreage	A
acceleration	A; G	acres	A
acceleration due to gravity	G	across	A; AC
		act	DORA; PACE; SEA
acceptable	OK; U		
acceptance	ACC; ACPT		
accepted	A	acting	A; ACT; ACTG

acting for	PP	adult-oriented rock	AOR
actinium	AC	advance	A; SUB
actinon	AN	advance purchase excursion	APEX
Action on Smoking and Health	ASH	advanced	A
active	A; ACT	advanced gas turbine	AGT
active control system	ACS	advanced gas-cooled reactor	AGR
active duty	AD		
Activity of Daily Living	ADL	advanced passenger train	APT
Actors' Benevolent Fund	ABF	advanced skills teacher	AST
actual bodily harm	ABH	advanced supersonic transport	AST
actual gross weight	AGW		
actual time of departure	ATD	advanced turboprop	ATP
		advantage	AD; VAN
actuaries	FA; IA	advent	ADV
actuary	AIA	adverb	ADV
acute respiratory disease	ARD	advert; advertisement	AD; ADVT
		advertisers	IPA; ISBA
ad infinitum	ADINF	advertising	PR
addendum; addition	ADD; PS	Advertising Standards Authority	ASA
additional	ADD		
additional postscript	PPS	advice of duration and charge	ADC
additional premium	AP		
additional voluntary contribution	AVC	advisory	ADV
		Advisory Board	AB
address	ADD; URL	Advisory Centre for Education	ACE
adjective	A; ADJ		
adjourned	ADJ	advocate	ADV
adjustment	ADJ	Aero Club	AC
adjutant	ADJ; ADJT	Aeronautical Research Council	ARC
adjutant-general	AG		
ad-men	*see* advertisers	aeroplane	*see* aircraft
administration	ADMIN	Afghanistan	AFG
administrative trainee	AT	Africa; African	AFR
admiral	ADM	African, Caribbean and Pacific	ACP
admiral of the fleet	AF		
admitting everybody	U	African Financial Community	CFA
adult	A; X		
		African National Congress	ANC

African Union	AU	Air Transport Association	ATA
after date	AD	Air Transport Auxiliary	ATA
after death	PM	air vice-marshal	AVM
after extra time	AET	airborne	AB
after midnight	AM	airborne early warning	AEW
afternoon	A; PM	air-chief-marshal	ACM
afters	PUD	air-conditioned; air-conditioning	AC
afterthought	PS		
again	DO; RE	aircraft	CTOL; EFA; HOTOL; ME; MIG; MRCA; QTOL; SST; STOL; VTOL
against	ADV; CON; V; VS		
against all risks	AAR		
aged	AE; AET		
agent	AGT; FED; REP		
agents	*see* spies	aircraft designers	MIG
agreed	OK	Aircraft Research Association	ARA
agreement	AGT; OK		
agriculturalist	*see* agriculturist	aircraftman; aircraftsman	AC; LAC
agriculture	AGR; AGRIC		
agriculturist	BAGR; BAGRIC; BAS	aircraftswoman; aircraftwoman	ACW; LACW
		air-ground-air	AGA
aide	PA	airline	BA; BAC; BEA; BM; BMI; BOAC; JAL; KLM; PANAM; PIA; SAS; TWA
aide-de-camp	ADC		
AIDS drug	AZT; Q		
AIDS-related complex	ARC		
ailment	*see* illness	airman	AC; ERK; FO; PO
Air Corps	AC	airman recruit	AR
air defence	AD	airmen	RAAF; RAF; RCAF; RFC; USAF
Air Efficiency Award	AE		
air force	RAF; USAF; WAAF; WRAAF; WRAF	airplane	*see* aircraft
		air-raid precautions	ARP
Air Force Cross	AFC	air-sea rescue	ASR
Air Force Medal	AFM	air-traffic control	ATC
Air Officer Commanding	AOC	aitch	H
		Alabama	AL; ALA
Air Police	AP	Alaska	AK; ALAS
air speed	AS	Alaska Standard Time; Alaska Time	AKST; AST
air staff	AS		
Air Training Corps	ATC	Albania	AL; ALB

Albert	AL	Alternative Investment Market	AIM
Albert Medal	AM	alternative technology	AT
Alberta	AB	alternative vote	AV
album-oriented rock	AOR	altitude	ALT
Alcoholics Anonymous	AA	alto	A; ALT
alderman	ALD; CA	aluminium	AL
Alderney	GBA	alumnus	OB
Alfred	ALF	always	EER
algebra; algebraic	ALG	Alzheimer's Disease	AD
Algeria	ALG; DZ	am	M
alias	AKA	amateur	A; AM
Alice; Alicia	ALI	amateur work	DIY
alien	ET	ambassador	HE
Alison; Alisson; Allison	ALI	America	A; AM; AMER; US; USA
alkalinity	PH	America Online	AOL
all	A	American	A; AM; AMER; US; USA
all agreed	NEMCON; NEMDISS	American Express®	AMEX
all correct	OK	American plan	AP
all items satisfactory	AOK	American shop	PX
all right	A1; OK	American Sign Language	ASL
all sections	AS	American soap	ER
Allied Command Europe	ACE	American soldier	GI
Allied Headquarters	AHQ	American Standards Association	ANSI; ASA
Allison	*see* Alison	American Stock Exchange	AMEX
all-points bulletin	APB	americium	AM
all-terrain vehicle	ATV	amid	MID
allure	SA	ammeter	A
alpha	A	Amnesty International	AI
alphabet	ABC; IPA; ITA	amount	AMT; QT; QTY
Alpine Club	AC	ampere	A; AMP
alright	A1; OK	ampere hour	AH
also called; also known as; also named	AKA	amplifier	AMP
alternate	ALT	amplitude modulation	AM
alternating current	AC		

anaesthetic	PCP	Anne	*see* Ann
anaesthetist	FRCA	anno Domini	AD
analgesic	PCP	announcement	AD
analogous	ANAL	annual equivalent rate	AER
analogue-to-digital	AD	annual percentage rate	APR
analogy	ANAL	annual return	AR
analysis	ANAL; SWOT	annualized percentage rate	APR
analytic; analytical	ANAL	anonymous	A; AN; ANON
anatomic; anatomy	ANAT	answer	A; ANS
ancient	ANC	answer, send and receive	ASR
ancient times	BC	ante	A; AN
anciently	ANC	ante meridiem	AM
and	N	anterior	A
and elsewhere	ETAL	anterior cruciate ligament	ACL
and others	ETAL	anti	CON; V; VS
and so forth	USW	anti-abortionists	SPUC
and so on	ETC	anti-aircraft	AA
and the rest	ETC	anti-aircraft artillery	AAA
and what follows	ETSEQ; ETSQ	anti-apartheid groups	UDF
Andorra	AD; AND	antidepressant	SSRI
Aneirin; Aneurin	NYE	antigen	PSA
Anglican	CE; COFE	anti-inflammatory agent	MSM
Anglo-French	AF	antimony	SB
Anglo-Latin	AL	Anti-Nazi League	ANL
Anglo-Norman	AN	anti-nuclear group	CND
Anglo-Saxon	AS	anti-personnel	AP
Angola	AN	antiquarian	ANTIQ; FAS
Ångström	A	antiquaries	SA; SAL; SAS
Ångström unit	AU	antiquary	FSA
angular momentum	L	antiques; antiquities	ANTIQ
Angus	GUS	antisubmarine	AS
animal	ROO	antisubmarine warfare	ASW
animal doctor	VET	anti-tank	AT
Animal Liberation Front	ALF	any number	N
Ann; Anna; Anne	NAN		
Annabel; Annabella; Annabelle	BEL		

any other business	AOB	arc tangent	ARCTAN
aorist	AOR	archaic	ARCH
apartment	APT	archaism	ARCH
Apocalypse	APOC	archbishop	ABP
apocrypha; apocryphal	APOC	archdeacon	ARCHD; VEN
Apocryphal Book	*see* Appendix: Books of the Bible	archduke	ARCHD
		archers	FITA
apogee	APO	archery	ARCH
apothecary	AP; LSA	archipelago	ARCH
apparent; apparently	AP; APP	architect	ARCH; ARCHIT; BARCH
appeal	SA; SOS		
appellation contrôlée; appellation d'origine contrôlée	AC; AOC; DOC	architects	AA; RIAS; RIBA
		Architects Registration Board	ARB
appendix	APP	architectural	ARCH; ARCHIT
applied	APP	Architectural Association	AA; RIAS; RIBA
apprentice	APP; L		
appropriate technology	AT	architecture	ARCH; ARCHIT
approval; approve	OK	archive	PRO
approved	APP	are	A; RE
approved driving instructor	ADI	area	A
		area of outstanding natural beauty	AONB
approximate	APP; APPROX		
approximately	A; APPROX; C; CA; CIR; CIRC	Argentina	RA
		arginine	ARG
April	APR; AV	argon	A; AR
aqueous	AQ	aristocratic	U
Arab	AR	arithmetic	ARITH; R
Arab Banking Corporation	ABC	arithmetic logic unit	ALU
		arithmetical	ARITH
Arabella	BEL	Arizona	ARIZ; AZ
Arabia; Arabian	AR; ARAB	Arkansas	AR; ARK
Arabic	AR; ARAB	Armenian	ARM
Aramaic	AR	Armoric	ARM
arbitrageur	ARB	armoured fighting vehicle	AFV
arbitrator	ACAS; REF; UMP		
arbitrators	ACAS	armoured personnel carrier	APC
arc cosine	ARCCOS		
arc sine	ARCSIN		

army	AA; AAC; ATS; AVR; BAOR; CA; CFE; GAR; INLA; IRA; SA; TA; TAVR; USA; WAAC; WRAAC; WRAC	as soon as possible	ASAP; PDQ
Army Air Corps	AAC	as the need arises	PRN
Army Benevolent Fund	ABF	Ascension Island	AC
army headquarters	AHQ	aspect ratio	AR
Army Order	AO	assistant	ASST; PA
army regulation	AR	assistant editor	SUB
Army Volunteer Reserve	AVR	assistant secretary	AS
around	A; APPROX; C; CA; CIR; CIRC	assistant stage manager	ASM
arranged; arranged by; arranger	ARR	associate	A; ASS; ASSOC
arrival; arrived; arrives; arriving	ARR	associate fellow	AF
		associate member	AM
arsenic	AS	Associate of Arts	AA
artery	*see* road	associated	ASS; ASSOC
article	A; ART	Associated British Cinemas	ABC
artificial	ART	Associated Press	AP
artificial insemination	AI; AID; AIH; DI	association	ASS; ASSOC
artificial intelligence	AI	astatine	AT
artillery	ART; ARTY; HA; RA; RHA	astronomer	ASTR; ASTRON
artist	ARA; ARSA; FAS; FRSA; RA	astronomers	RAS
		astronomical	ASTR; ASTRON
artists	ICA; RA; RSA; RWS	astronomical unit(s)	AU
arts council	ACE; ACGB; ACNI; ACW; SAC	astronomy	ASTR; ASTRON
		at pleasure	ADLIB
as	EG	at the beginning	ADINIT
as a favour	EXGR	at the end	ADFIN
as above	US; UTSUP	at the place	ADLOC
as an act of grace	EXGR	at the suit of	ATS
as much as you please	QL	at this place	AHL
as much as you wish	QV	at this word	AHV
as said	UTDICT	at will	ADLIB
		athletes	AAA; AAC; AC; BAF
		athletic	A
		athletic club	AC
		Atlantic Standard Time; Atlantic Time	AST; AT

full form ⇨ abbreviation

atmosphere; atmospheric	ATM	author's proof	AP
atomic	A	autobahn	AB
Atomic Energy Authority	AEA	autobiography	CV
		automatic data processing	ADP
Atomic Energy Commission	AEC	automatic direction-finder	ADF
atomic mass unit	AMU	automatic flight control	AFC
atomic number	ATNO; ATNUMB; Z	automatic gain control	AGC
Atomic Weapons Establishment	AWE	automatic message routeing	AMR
atomic weight	A; ATWT	automatic public convenience	APC
atomic weight unit	AWU	automatic send and receive	ASR
Attachment Unit Interface	AUI	automatic station tuning	AST
attorney	ATT; ATTY; DA	automatic teller machine	ATM
Attorney-General	AG	automatic train control	ATC
attributed; attributive; attributively	ATTRIB	automatic train protection	ATP
audio-frequency	AF	automatic vehicle identification	AVI
audio-frequency modulation	AFM	automatic vending machine	AVM
audiovisual	AV	automatic volume control	AVC
audiovisual aid(s)	AVA	automobile	*see* car
Audit Bureau of Circulations	ABC	Automobile Association	AA
augmentative	AUG; AUGM	autonomic nervous system	ANS
August	AUG	autonomous region	AR
Augustinian(s)	OSA	auxiliaries	ATA; ATS; RFA; WAAC; WAAF; WRAC; WRAF
Augustus	GUS		
Auntie	BBC		
Australasia	AASIA		
Australia	A; AUS; AUST; AUSTR; OZ		
Australian	A; AUST; AUSTR; OZ	avenue	AV; AVE
Australian Army	AA	average	AV; AVE
Austria	A	average annual rainfall	AAR
authorization	OK	avoiding drink	TT
authorized version	AV		

full form ➪ abbreviation

award	AE; CH; NTA; OBE; OM; *see also* Appendix: Decorations	axis	X; Y; Z
		Azed	AZ
		Azerbaijan	AZ
axiom	AX	azidothymidine	AZT

B

B natural	H	baritone	BAR
baby	SIS	barium	BA
baccalaureate	BAC	baron	B; BN
bachelor	B; BA; BACH; *see also* Appendix: Degrees	baronet	BART; BT
		barracks	BKS
Bachelor of Arts	AB; BA	barrel	B; BL
Bachelor of Medicine	MB	barrels	B; BBL
Bachelor of Science	BSC	barrister	BAR; KC; QC
Bach's works	BWV	barristers	ABA
bacteria; bacterium	ECOLI; MRSA	Barry	BAZ
badge	ID	barter system	LETS
The Bahamas	BS	Bartholomew	BAT
Bahrain	BRN	Baruch	BAR
balance	BAL	baryon number	B
balance sheet	BS	base	E
bale	BL	baseball statistic	ERA
ball	O	basic input-output system	BIOS
band	CB		
Bangladesh	BD	Basil	BAZ
bank	BIS; BK; EBRD; ECB; EIB; HSBC; IBRD; TSB	basketball association	NBA
		Basque separatists	ETA
		bass	B
bank draft	BD	battalion	BAT; BATT; BN
Bank for International Settlements	BIS	battery	BAT; BATT
		battery commander	BC
bank rate	BR; LIBOR	Bavarian Motor Works	BMW
banker	ACIB; AIB; FCIB	beak	JP
bankers	AIB; BBA; BIFU; CIB	beam	RSJ
		bearing	E; N; NE; NW; S; SE; SW; W
banking	BKG		
banks	CFP	Beatrice; Beatrix	BEA; BEE
Baptist	BAP; BAPT	beats per minute	BPM
baptized	BAP; BAPT	becoming gradually slower	RALL; RIT
Barbados	BDS		
Barbara	BAB	becoming louder	CRESC
barbecue	BBQ	becoming quieter	DIM; DIMIN
the Bard	WS	becquerel(s)	BQ
Bardot	BB	bed and breakfast	BANDB; BB
		bedbug	B

Bedfordshire	BEDS	big cheese; big noise; big shot; bigwig	VIP
bedroom	BR	bigwigs	EPG
bee	B	bill	AC; AD; IOU; *see also* account
Beethoven's works	WOO		
Beetle	VW	bill of exchange	BE
before	A; AN; BEF	bill of lading	BL
before a meal	AP	bill of sale	BS
before Christ	AC; BC	billion	B; BN
before food	AC	billion electronvolts	BEV
before 1950	BP	bills discounted	BD
before noon	AM	bills payable	BP
before present	BP	bills receivable	BR
before the Common Era	BCE	binary coded decimal	BCD
		binary digit	BIT
before the day	AD	biography	BIO; CV
beginner	DEB; L	biology	BIOL
beginning of year	JAN	bird protectors	RSPB
Belarus	BY	Birkenhead	FE
Belgian	BELG	birthday	DOB
Belgium	B; BELG	birthplace	BP; BPL
Belize	BH; BZ	bisexual	BI
below	INF	bishop	B; BP; RR
bend	S; U; Z	bismuth	BI
Benedictine(s)	OSB	bits per inch	BPI
Benin	DY	bits per second	BPS
Benjamin	BEN	black	B
berkelium	BK	black and white	BW
Berkshire	BERKS	Blessed Virgin	BV
beryllium	BE	Blessed Virgin Mary	BVM
best	A1; NO1	blind carbon copy	BCC
betting	SP	blob	O
between	BET	blood alcohol level	BAL
Bible	AV; BIB; EV; NEB; NT; OT; RSV; RV	blood group	A; AB; B; O
		blood pressure	BP
biblical	BIBL	blood relative	*see* relation
bibliographical; bibliography	BIBL	bloody fool	BF
		blue jacket	AB; OS; TAR
big	OS	board	BD; EXEC

board member	EXEC	boots	DMS
board of control	BC	boozer	PH
Board of Education	BE	born	B; N; NAT
Board of Trade unit	BTU	boron	B
boarder	PG	borough	BOR
boat	CAT; MTB; MV; MY; SS; TB; U; ULCC	Bosnia and Herzegovina	BIH
bob	S	boss	CEO; ED; MD
bobby	*see* policeman	botanical; botany	BOT
body	BOD	Botswana	RB
body mass index	BMI	bottle	BOT
body odour	BO	boulevard	BLVD; BOUL
bodyguard	SS	bounce	RD
bog	*see* toilet	bound	BD
bohemian	BOHO	boundary	IV; VI
bohrium	BH	bounder	ROO
boilers, radiators, *etc*	CH	bowled	B
boiling point	BP	box	TV
boiling-water reactor	BWR	box office	BO
bold face	BF	boxer	ROO
Bolivia	BOL	boxers	ABA; EBU; IBF; NBA; WBA; WBC; WBO
Boltzmann constant	K	boy	B; *see also* Appendix: First Names
bomb	A; H; V1		
bombardier	BDR	Boys' Brigade	BB
bomber	B	brace	PR
bond	BD	brain scanner	PET
bond picker; bondsman	ERNIE	brake horsepower	BHP
Bond's boss	M	braking system	ABS
bone	T	branch	BR
bones	*see* doctor	branch office	BO
book	B; BK; LIB; TOM; V; VOL; *see also* Appendix: Books of the Bible	brassière	BRA
		bravo	B
book of knowledge	ENCY; ENCYC; ENCYCL	Brazil	BR; BRAZ
		Brazilian	BRAZ
books	BB; BKS; NT; OT	bread	L; LSD; P
booksellers	BA	breadth	B

breakdown service	AA; RAC	British Standards	BS
bridge	BR	British Summer Time	BST
bridge pair; bridge partners	*see* partners	British troops	*see* Appendix: Armed Services
bridge player	*see* player	Briton	BRIT
bridge opponents	*see* opponents	broadcasters	ABC; ATV; BBC; BECTU; BFBS; CBC; CNN; EBU; ITV; LBC; LWT; NBC; RCA; RTE; SABC; SSVC; STV; VOA
brigade	BDE		
brigadier	BRIG		
Brigitte Bardot	BB		
bring your own	BYO		
bring your own beer; bring your own booze; bring your own bottle	BYOB		
		broadcasting system	PAL; SECAM
		brokers	BIBA
Britain	B; BR; BRIT; GB; UK	bromine	BR
		bronze	BR
Britannia	BRIT	brother	BR; BRO; DOM
British	B; BR; BRIT; UK	brotherhood	FRAT
British Academy	BA	brothers	BROS; *see also* monk(s)
British Aerospace	BAE		
British Airports Authority	BAA	brought forward	BF
		brown	BR
British Antarctic Survey	BAS	brown shirts	SA
		Brunei	BRU
British Columbia	BC	Buckinghamshire	BUCKS
British Computer Society	BCS	budgerigar	BUDGE; BUDGIE
		bug	FLU; MRSA
British Council	BC	building	BLDG
British Deaf Association	BDA	Building Societies Commission	BSC
British Empire Medal	BEM	building society	BS
British Expeditionary Force	BEF	Bulgaria	BG; BULG
		Bulgarian	BULG
British Honduras	BH	bulletin board system	BBS
British Legion	BL		
British Library	BL	Burkina Faso	BF
British Museum	BM	Burlington House	RA
British Rail	BR	Burundi	RU
British Road Services	BRS	bus	USB
British School of Motoring	BSM	bushel(s)	BU

full form ⇨ abbreviation

business	BIZ; BUS; *see also* company	by proxy	PERPRO; PP
		by reason of death	CM
business course	MBA	by the agency of another	PERPRO; PP
Business Expansion Scheme	BES		
		by the grace of God	DG
Business Software Alliance	BSA	by the thousand	PERMIL
		by the way	BTW; OB
Butler	RAB	by virtue of office	EXOFF
buy one get one free	BOGOF	by virtue of position	EXOFF
buyer's option	BO	bytes per inch	BPI
by	X		

cabinet maker	PM	cancer	KS
cadmium	CD	candela	CD
Caernarvonshire	CAERNS	candle-power	CP
caesium	CS	canine	C
calcium	CA	canon	CAN
calendar	CAL	Canterbury	CANT; CANTUAR
calibre	CAL	canticles	CANT
California	CA; CAL; CALIF	canto	CAN
californium	CF	canton	CAN
call for help	SOS	cap	TAM
calorie	C; CAL	capacitance	C
Cambodia	K	capacity	CAP
Cambridge	CAMB	cape	C
Cambridge: of Cambridge	CANTAB	Cape Colony	CC
		Cape Coloured	CC
Cambridgeshire	CAMB; CAMBS	capital	A1; CAP; KL; UC
camera	SLR	capital account	CA
camera cassette recorder	CCR	capital expenditure	CAPEX
		capital gains tax	CGT
camera-ready copy	CRC	capital letter	CAP
Cameroon	CAM	capital letters	CAPS; UC
Campaign Against Nuclear Dumping	CAND	capital transfer tax	CTT
		capitalize	CAP
Campaign Against Racial Discrimination	CARD	capitals	*see* capital letters
		Capone	AL
Campaign for Lead-free Air	CLEAR	caps	UC
		captain	CAPT; SKIP
Campaign for Nuclear Disarmament	CND	captain of the guard	CG
		captain-general	CG
Campaign for Real Ale	CAMRA	captive	POW
can	*see* toilet	caput	c
Canada; Canadian	CAN; CDN	car	BMW; CAB; GT; GTI; JAG; MG; RR; T; VW
Canadian National	CN		
Canadian province	AB; BC; MB; NB; NF; NS; NT; NW; ON; PE; PQ; Q; QUE; SK; YT	car manufacturers	BL; BMW; GM; MG; RR; VW
		car theft	TWOC
canal	CAN	carat	C; CT; K
Canberra	CAN	caravan	VAN
cancellation; cancelled	CANC		

C

full form ⇨ abbreviation

carbon	C	catalogue of Schubert's works	D
carbon copies; carbon copy	CC	cataloguing in publication	CIP
carbon dioxide	COO	cataloguing in source	CIS
carbon monoxide	CO	catalytic converter	CAT
card	A; J; K; PC; Q	catamaran	CAT
card game	NAP	catapult	Y
Cardiganshire	CARDS	catechism	CAT
cardinal	CARD; HE	caterpillar	CAT
cardinal point	E; N; S; W	Catharine; Catherina; Catherine	KAY; KIT
care of	C; CO	cathedral	CATH
cargo transport	C	Catherina; Catherine	*see* Catharine
Caribbean	CARIBB; WI	cathode	CATH
Caribbean Community	CARICOM	cathode-ray oscilloscope	CRO
Carmen	*see* driving club	cathode-ray tube	CRT
carriage	CGE	Catholic	C; CATH; RC
carriage return	CR	caught	C; CT
carriage-forward	CGEFWD	caught and bowled; caught and bowled by	CANDB
carriage-paid	CGEPD	caught by	C; CT
carried down	CD	Cecilia; Cecily; Cicely	CIS
carried forward	CF	celebrated	CEL
cart	T	Celsius	C
case	ABL; ACC; ACCUS; DAT; GEN; NOM; OBJ; SUBJ; VOC	Celtic	CELT
		cent	C; CT
cases	CA	centigrade	C; CENT
cash before delivery	CBD	centigram(s); centigramme(s)	CG
cash discount	CD	centilitre(s)	CL
cash on delivery	COD	centimes	C
cash with order	CWO	centimetre(s)	CM
castle	R	centimetre-gram-second	CGS
catalogue	CAT; K	central	CEN; CENT
catalogue of Bach's works	BWV	Central African Republic	RCA
catalogue of Beethoven's works	WOO	Central America	CA
catalogue of Mozart's works	K		
catalogue of Scarlatti's works	K		

full form	abbreviation	full form	abbreviation
Central Control Function	CCF	chamber	PO
Central European Time	CET; MEZ	chamber of commerce	COFC
central heating	CH	chamberlain	CHAMB
central nervous system	CNS	chamberpot	PO
Central Office of Information	COI	Chambers	C
Central Policy Review Staff	CPRS	champion	CH
		chancellor	CE; CHANC
central processing unit	CPU	chancery	CHANC
Central Standard Time	CST	Channel Islands	CI
Central Time	CT	chaplain	CF; CH; CHAP; HCF; OCF
centre of buoyancy	CB	chapter	C; CAP; CH; CHAP
centre of gravity	CG		
centre-forward	CF	chapters	CC
centre-half	CH	characters per inch	CPI
century	C; CEN; CENT	characters per minute	CPM
cerebrospinal fluid	CSF	characters per second	CPS
cerebrovascular accident	CVA	charge	CHG
		Charge Advice	ADC
cerium	CE	charge-coupled device	CCD
certainly	OK; OKE	Charles	CAR
certificate	CERT; CERTED; CERTIF; COFA; COP; CPVE; CSE; GCE; GCSE; HNC; MOT; NCEA; ONC; SC; SCE; U	Charlie	C
		chart	CH
		chartered accountant	*see* accountant
		chartered engineer	CENG
		chartered surveyor	CS
Certificate of Proficiency	COP	chauvinist	MCP
certificated; certified	CERT; CERTIF	check	CH
certified nursery nurse	CNN	checkmate	CHM
certify	CERT; CERTIF	cheese	VIP
Ceylon	CL	chelating agent	EDTA
Chad	TCH	chemical	CHEM; *see also* Appendix: Chemical Elements
chain	CH		
chair	MC; PROF		
chairman	CHM; CHMN; MC; PROF	chemical engineer	CE; CHE
		chemical warfare	CW
chairperson; chairwoman	MC; PROF	chemical weapons convention	CWC

C

chemically pure	CP	Christian Science	CS
chemist	FCS; LSA; MPS; RIC	Christian times	AD
		Christmas	XM
chemistry	CHEM	Christmas period	DEC
chemistry society	RSC	Christopher	KIT
Cheshire	CHES	chromium	CR
chestnut	CH	chromosome	X; Y
chevaux	CV	chronic fatigue syndrome	CFS; ME
chevron	V		
chief	CH; ED	chronic heart failure	CCF
chief accountant	CA	chronic wasting disease	CWD
chief engineer	CE	chronicle	CHRON
Chief Intelligence Directorate	GRU	Chronicles	CH; CHRON
		chronological; chronology	CHRON
Chief Justice	CHJ		
Chief of General Staff	CGS	chrysanthemum	MUM
Chief of Staff	COFS; COS	church	CE; CH; COFE; COFI; COFS; EC; ECUSA; FC; PE; RC; RCC; RE; REFCH; RP; UF; UP; URC
Chief of the Imperial General Staff	CIGS		
Chief Petty Officer	CPO		
child	CH		
Child Poverty Action Group	CPAG	Church Army	CA
		Church Mission Society	CMS
Child Support Agency	CSA		
childbirth trust	NCT	Church of England	CE; COFE
childless	SP	Church of Ireland	COFI
children	CH	Church of Scotland	COFS
Chile	RCH	churchman	*see* clergyman
China; Chinese	CH; CHIN	Cicely	*see* Cecilia
chip	IC; ULA	cipher	O
chiropodist	SRCH	circa	C; CA
chiropractor	DC	circle	O
chit	IOU	circuit	AND; IC; NAND; NOR; NOT; O; OR
chlorine	CL		
choir	CH		
Christ	CH; CHR; X; XT	circular letter	O
Christian	CHR; RC; XN; XTIAN	citation	CIT
		citizen	CIT
Christian era	AD	Citizens' Advice Bureau	CAB

Citizens' Band	CB	closed-circuit television	CCTV
city	EC; KL; LA; NY; RIO	cloudy	C
City and Guilds Institute	CANDG; CGI	club	AA; AAC; AC; AELTC; AFC; BUNAC; CC; CCC; CTC; FC; MCC; RAC; RANDA
civil	CIV		
Civil Aviation Authority	CAA		
civil defence	CD	clubhouse	CH
Civil Defence Volunteer; Civil Defence Volunteers	CDV	clubs	C
		coadjutor	COAD
		coastguard	CG
civil engineer	CE	coat	MAC
civil justice	CJ	coat-card	J; K; Q
civil service	CS	cobalt	CO
Civil Service Commission	CSC	cocaine	C
		codex	COD
civilian	CIV	codicil	PS
clairvoyance	ESP	coefficient of drag	CD
class	CL	coenzyme	NAD
classical	CLASS	cognate	COG
classification	A; AA; CLASS; G; PG; R; U; X	cohabitee; cohabiter	SOP
Classification of Residential Neighbourhoods	ACORN®	coin	CR; D; F; FL; P; S; SOV
		cold	C
classy	U	Coldstream Guards	CG
cleaner	VAC	collateral; collaterally	COLLAT
clearing house	CH	colleague	COLL
clef	C; F; G	collect on delivery	COD
clergyman; clergywoman	ABP; ARCHD; BP; CHAP; DD; MGR; MIN; MONSIG; MSGR; P; PP; PR RECT; REV; REVD; RR; RTREV; VEN; VIC; VREV	collection of books	NT; OT
		collective; collector	COLL
		college	C; CAT; CFE; COLL; LSE; *see also* Appendix: Colleges
		colloquial	COLL; COLLOQ
cleric	*see* clergyman	colloquially	COLLOQ
Clerk to the Signet	CS	cologarithm	COLOG
close	CLO	Colombia	CO
closed-circuit	CC	colonel	COL

full form ⇨ abbreviation

Colorado	CO; COL; COLO	commodore	CDRE; COM
Colossians	COL; COLOSS	common	COM
colour	COL	Common Agricultural Policy	CAP
colour graphics adapter	CGA		
coloured	C	common entrance	CE
colt	C	Common Era	CE
columbium	CB	Common Fisheries Policy	CFP
column	COL		
Combined Cadet Force	CCF	common market	CACM; CARICOM; ECOWAS; EEC
combined heat and power	CHP		
combined operations	CO	Common Prayer	CP
Combined Services Entertainment	CSE	common time	C
		commoner	MP
comedy	COM	commonwealth	COM
comic	MAG	Commonwealth of Independent States	CIS
command paper	C; CD; CM; CMD; CMND		
		Commonwealth Office	CO
command post	CP	commune	COM
commandant	COMDT	communication	COMM; FAX
commander	CBE; CDR; CINC; CMDR; CO; COM; COMDR; COMM; GOC; OC	communication system	UMTS
		Communication Workers Union	CWU
commander-in-chief	CIC; CINC	communications intelligence	COMINT
commanding general	CG		
commanding officer	CO; OC	communist	COM
commandos	SAS	Communist Party	CP
commentary	COMM	community	CACM; CARICOM; CFA; CR; EC; ECOWAS; ECSC; EDC; EEC
commerce	COM		
commercial	*see* advert		
commercial fast reactor	CFR	community-service order	CSO
		community-service volunteer	CSV
commission	COMMN		
commissioner	COM; COMR	companion	AC; BUD; CB; CCMI; CDSO; CH; CIE; CLIT; CLITT; CMG
committee	COM		
Committee of State Security	KGB		
		Companion of Honour	CH
Committee on Safety of Medicines	CSM	Companion of Literature	CLIT; CLITT

full form ⇨ abbreviation

Companion of the Bath	CB
company	ABC; AG; BASF; BL; BP; BV; CIA; CIE; CO; COY; EMI; ESSO; GE; GEC; GKN; GMBH; GUS; HBC; IBM; ICI; ITT; LBC; LONRHO; MMM; NBC; OEIC; PANDO; PLC; PRU; REC; RSC; RTZ; SA; TNT; TOC
comparative	COMP; COMPAR
compare	CF; COMP; CP
comparison	COMPAR
compère	MC
Competition Commission	CC
compiler	COMP; CP
compliance	C
composer	COMP
composite rate tax	CRT
composition	OP
compound	COMP; CPD
compound annual rate	CAR
compound net annual rate	CNAR
compounded	COMP
compounded annual rate	CAR
comprehensive	COMP; ENCY; ENCYC; ENCYCL
comprising	COMP
compulsory competitive tendering	CCT
computational fluid dynamics	CFD
computer	ERNIE; MPC; NC; PC; RISC
computer game	MUD

computer input on microfilm	CIM
computer integrated manufacture	CIM
computer interface	WIMP
computer language recorder	CLR
computer language translator	CLT
computer output on microfilm	COM
computer store	*see* memory
computer studies	IT
computer system	BIOS; CPM; DDE; DOS; GIS; MSDOS®
computer technology	IT
computer-aided design	CAD
computer-aided drafting	CAD
computer-aided engineering	CAE
computer-aided instruction	CAI
computer-aided learning	CAL
computer-aided manufacture; computer-aided manufacturing	CAM
computer-aided production	CAP
computer-aided training	CAT
computer-assisted learning	CAL
computer-assisted training	CAT
computer-based information system	CBIS
computer-based training	CBT

C

full form ⇨ abbreviation

computer-managed instruction	CMI	Congregation of the Passion	CP
computer-managed learning	CML	congregational	CONG
		congress	CONG
computer-operated electronic display	COED	Congress of Industrial Organizations	CIO
computer-orientated language	COL	Congress of Racial Equality	CORE
computing	IT	congressional	CONG
concentrated; concentration	CONC	conjunction	CONJ
		conjunctive	CONJ
concerning	RE	connected	CONN
conchie; conchy	CO	Connecticut	CONN; CT
conclusion	CON	connection	CONN
Concorde	SST	conscientious objector	CO
condition	AD; AIDS; ALS; ARD; CHD; CJD; COPD; CWD; DI; DM; DS; FMD; GVHD; KS; ME; MND; MS; NVCJD; PCP; PID; SCID; STD; TB; TSE; VD	consecrated	CONS
		conservation	CON
		conservationists	ACE; BTCV; CPRE; FOE; NT; NTS; RSNC; RSPB; SPAB
		conservative	C; CON; CONS
conductance	G	consigned; consignment	CONS
Confederate States of America	CSA	consolidated	CONS
		consonant	CONS
Confederation of British Industry	CBI	constable	CONS; PC; WPC
confer	CF	Constance	CON
confidence	CON	constant	C; CONST; E; F; G; H; K; P; R
confined to barracks	CB	constant of gravitation	G
confined to camp	CC	constitution	CONS; CONST
confinement	CB	constitutional	CONS
confirmation	OK	construction	CONS; CONSTR
conformist	CON	construction workers	UCATT
congestion	C	consul	CON
Congo: Democratic Republic of	CGO; ZRE	consul general	CG
		consular agent	CA
Congo: Republic of	RCB	consulting	CONS
congregation	CONG	consumer council	NCC
Congregation of the Mission	CM		

consumer price index	CPI
Consumers' Association	CA
consumption	TB
contagious disease(s)	CD
contemporary	AD
continued	CONT; CONTD
continuous variable transmission	CVT
contraceptive	IUCD; IUD
contracted	CONTR
contraction	CONTR; Z
contralto	C
controlled drug	CD
convenience	see toilet
convict	CON
cooker	AGA
co-ordinate	X; Y; Z
cop	see policeman
copper	CU; D; F; P; see also policeman
coppers	D; P; see also police
copy	FAX; MS
copyright	C
Corinthians	COR
corner	COR; NE; NW; SE; SW
cornet	COR
Cornish	CORN
Cornwall	CORN; SW
corollary	COROL
coronary artery bypass graft	CABG
coronary care unit	CCU
coronary heart disease	CHD
Coronary Prevention Group	CPG
coroner	COR
corporal	CORP; CPL; NCO

corporation	CORP
corps	C; RAC; REME; ROC
correct	OK; U
correspond	CORR
corresponding	CORRES
corresponding member	CM
corrupted; corruption	CORR
cosecant	COSEC
cosine	COS
cost and freight	CAF; CANDF; CF
cost, freight and insurance	CFANDI
cost, freight, insurance	CFI
cost, insurance, freight	CIF
Costa Rica	CR
cost-of-living adjustment	COLA
cotangent	COT
Côte d'Ivoire	CI
coulomb	C
Council of Europe	CE; COE; COFE
councillor	CLLR; CR
county	CO; see also Appendix: Counties of England and Wales
county alderman	CA
county borough	CB
county council	CC
county councillor	CC
county cricket club	CCC
couple	PR
course	EST; PPE; SEM
course of life	CV
court	CS; CT
court card	J; K; Q
court house	CH
Court of Session	CS

full form	abbreviation	full form	abbreviation
cousin	COZ	crossword	XWD; XWORD
covariance	COV	crown	CR
Covent Garden	ROH	Crown Office	CO
coversed sine	COVERS	Crown Prosecution Service	CPS
coxswain	COX	cry for help	SOS
craft, design, technology	CDT	Cuba	C
craftsman	*see* sailor	cubic	C; CU; CUB
craniosacral therapy	CST	cubic centimetre(s)	CC
cream	UHT	cubic feet	CFT
credit	CR; HP	cubic feet of gas	CFG
credit account	CA	cubic foot	CFT
credit card	AMEX	cue	Q
credit note	CN; IOU	cultivar; cultivated variety	CV
creditor	CR	Cumbria	CUMB
crescendo	CRESC	curie	CI
crescent	CRES	curium	CM
crew member	*see* sailor	current	AC; CUR; CURT; DC; I
cricket board	ECB	current account	CA
cricket club	CC; CCC; MCC	current measure	AMP
cricketers	ICC; 11; MCC; XI	current purchasing power	CPP
crime prevention officer	CPO	curriculum council	NCC
criminal conversation	CRIMCON	curriculum vitae	CV
Criminal Records Office	CRO	customs house	CH
critical	CRIT	cycles per second	CPS; CS
critical compression ratio	CCR	cyclists	BCF; CTC; UCI
criticism	CRIT	Cyclists' Touring Club	CTC
Croatia	HR	cyclonite	RDX
Croix de Guerre	CG	Cymric	CYM
croquet club	AELTC; CC	Cyprus	CY
cross	X	Cyrus	CY
Cross of Valour	CV	Czech koruna	KC
cross-dresser	TV	Czech Republic	CZ
crossover value	COV		

D

da capo	DC	days after date	DD
dad; daddy	DA; PA; POP	day's date	DD
Dafydd	DAI	dead	D; DEC; EX; OB
Dahomey	DY	dead on arrival	DOA
daily	FT	dead-letter office	DLO
dal segno	DS	dead-weight tonnage	DWT
dalasi	GMD	dealer	DLR
dame	AD; DBE; DCB; DCMG; DCVO	Dean	RD
		Deanna; Deanne	DI; DIE
damn	D; DEE	Deborah; Debra	DEB
danger of explosion	HERO	debt	IOU
Daniel	DAN	debtor	DR
Danish	DAN	debutante	DEB
dark	DK	decalitre(s)	DAL
darling	HON	decametre(s)	DAM
data	GEN	deceased	D; DEC; EX; OB
data and telecommunications	DATEC	December	DEC
		decibel(s)	DB
data interchange format	DIF	decigram(s); decigramme(s)	DG
data processing	DP	decilitre(s)	DL
Data Protection Authority	DPA	decimetre(s)	DM
		decisive blow	KO
data transmission	DT	deck	DK
database	GRID	deck-hand	*see* sailor
datacommunications	DATACOMMS	declaration	DEC; UDI
date	D	declension	DEC; DECL
date of availability	DOA	decoration	DSO; GC; MBE; MC; MM; OBE; OM; TD; VC; *see also* Appendix: Decorations
date of birth	DOB		
dative	DAT		
daughter	D; DAU		
Daughters of the American Revolution	DAR		
		dee	D
David	DAI	deejay	DJ
day	D; FRI; MON; SAT; SUN; THU; THUR; THURS; TUES; VE; VJ; WED	deep-vein thrombosis	DVT
		defamation	SCANMAG
		defence	CD
		Defence Intelligence	DI
daylight saving time	DST	defendant	DEF; DFT

27

full form ⇨ abbreviation

defender of the faith	DF; FD; FIDDEF	department	D; DCMS; DE; DEA; DEFRA; DENI; DEP; DEPT; DETR; DFES; DFID; DFT; DH; DHSS; DOD; DOE; DOH; DPT; DSS; DTI; DTLR; DWP; FO; SSD
definition	DEF		
degree	BA; D; DEG; MA; *see also* Appendix: Degrees		
degree of acidity; degree of alkalinity	PH		
degrees	DEG		
Delaware	DE; DEL	departs	D; DEP
delegate	DEL	department store	*see* store
delete	D	departure	DEP
delirium; delirium tremens	DT; DTS	depleted uranium	DU
delivery	DLVY	deposed	DEP
delta	D	deposit	DEP
demand loan	DL	depression	PND; SAD
demilitarized zone	DMZ	depth	D; F
Democrat; Democratic	D; DEM	deputy	DEP; DEPT
demolish	KO	Deputy Lieutenant	DL
Denis; Dennis; Denys	DEN	deputy to the Dáil	TD
Denmark	DK	Derek; Derrick; Deryck	DEL
Dennis	*see* Denis		
density	D	derivation; derivative; derived	DER; DERIV
dent	V		
dental	DENT	Derrick; Deryck	*see* Derek
dentist	BDS; DDS; DENT; LDS; MDS; MDSC	descendant of	O
		deserted	AWOL; D
dentistry	DENT	designated driver	DD
dentists	BDA; GDC; RADC	designation of wines	AOC; DOC; DOCG
Denys	*see* Denis	designed: he/she designed	INV
deoxyribonucleic acid	DNA		
depart	D; DEP	designer drug	GHB
departed	D; DEC; EX; OB	desktop publishing	DTP
		dessert	PUD
		detainee	POW
		detective	DC; DCI; DET; DI; DS; PI; TEC
		detective inspector	DI
		detectives	CID; FBI; FEDS

detector	ASR; MTD; RDF; SAR	diminuendo	DIM; DIMIN
deuterium	D	diminutive	DIM; DIMIN
Deuteronomy	DEUT	dinar	D; DA; DNR; KD
Deutsch	D	dinner jacket	DJ
Deutschmark	DM; DMARK	dioptre	DPT
development agency	WDA	diploma	DIP; HND; OND; *see also* Appendix: Degrees
devised: he/she devised	INV		
Devon	SW	diplomat	CD; HE
diabetes	DI; DM	diplomats; diplomatic corps	CD
dialect	DIAL		
dialling	IDD; ISD; STD	direct current	DC
diameter	D; DIA; DIAM	direct debit	DD
diamonds	D	direct memory access	DMA
Dian; Diana; Diane; Dianne	DI; DIE	direction	E; ENE; ESE; L; N; NE; NNE; NNW; NW; R; S; SE; SSE; SSW; SW; W; WNW; WSW
dictation	DICT		
dictator	DICT		
dictionary	DICT; DNB; NODE; OED; TCD		
		direction finder	DF
		directly observed therapy, short-course	DOTS
did	D		
did: he/she did	FEC	director	D; DIR; DPP; DSS
did: they did	FF	director-general	DG
died	D; DEC; EX; OB	dirty old man	DOM
died without issue	DSP; OSP	disability living allowance	DLA
dietary reference values	DRV		
		disability-adjusted life year	DALY
difference; different	DIFF		
digit	I; V	Disablement Income Group	DIG
digital audio broadcasting	DAB		
		Disasters Emergency Committee	DEC
digital compact cassette	DCC		
		disc	CAD; CD; CDI; CDR; CDROM; CDRW; DVD; EP; ICD; LP; O; WORM
digital data storage	DDS		
digital subscriber line	DSL		
digital-to-analogue	DA	disc jockey	DJ
dignitary	VIP	Discharged Prisoners' Aid	DPA
dilute	DIL		
dimension	D; DIM	discontinued	DIS

full form ⇨ abbreviation

discount	DISC	divorced wife	EX
discounted cash flow	DCF	do	CON; UT
discourse	DISS	do not resuscitate	DNR
discoverer	DISC	dock	DK
disease	*see* illness	doctor	BM; DOC; DR;
disk	*see* disc		GP; MB; MD;
disk operating system	DOS; MSDOS®		MO; VET; *see also*
disks	RAID		surgeon *and*
dismissal; dismissed	B; C; CANDB;		Appendix: Degrees
	HW; LB; LBW;	Doctor of Divinity	DD
	RO; ST	Doctor of Medicine	MD
disorder	*see* illness	doctors	AMA; BMA;
displaced person	DP		GMC; MWF;
displacement	D		RAMC; RCGP;
disrespect	DIS		RCP
distance	DIST	document signed	DS
distant early warning	DEW	dog	LAB; POM; PUP
distilled	DIST	doh	UT
distinction	CH; MBE; OBE;	do-it-yourself	DIY
	OM; *see also*	dolce	DOL
	Appendix:	dole	FIS; JSA
	Decorations	dollar	D; DOL; S
distinguish	DIST	domain name system	DNS
distress signal	SOS	domestic	DOM
distributed array	DAP	dominee	DO
processor		Dominica	WD
district	DC; DIST	Dominical	DOM
district attorney	DA	Dominican	DOM; OP
district commissioner	DC	Dominican Republic	DOM
district court martial	DCM	Dominicans	OP
district medical officer	DMO	dominion	DOM; NZ
District of Columbia	DC	Donald	DON
district officer	DOC	donated	DD
commanding		donor insemination	DI
ditto	DO	doodlebug	V1
divide; dividend	DIV	dope	GEN; INF; *see*
divine	DD; DIV		*also* drug
divinity	RE; RI	Doric	DOR
division	DIV	Dorothea; Dorothy	DO; DOT
divorce; divorced	DIV	Dorset	DORS

dots per inch	DPI	drug abuse conference	SCODA
double	DBL	Drug Enforcement Administration	DEA
double-glazing	UPVC	drugs	PHARM
dough	L; LSD; P	drummer	DR
doughboy	GI	drunk and disorderly	DANDD
down	D; DN	dry	TT
down under	*see* Australia	dry riser	DR
dozen	DOZ; DZ; XII	dual in-line memory module	DIMM
drachma	DR	dubnium	DB
draft	DFT; MS	duck	O
dram	DR	Dudley	DUD
drama school	RADA	duff	NG
dramatist	GBS; WS	duke	D
drawer	DR	duplicate	DUP
drew: he/she drew	DEL	Durham	DUR
drill	PE; PT	Durham: of Durham	DUNELM
drink	GANDT; IT	Dutch	D; DU; UX; W
drive	DR; DV	Dutch company	BV
driver	DR	dwelling	HO; HSE
drivers	AA; AAA; RAC	dynamic data exchange	DDE
driving club	AA; RAC	dynamic link library	DLL
driving instructor	ADI	dynamite	TNT
driving instructors	BSM	dynamo	DYN
Driving Standards Agency	DSA	dynamometer	DYN
driving under the influence	DUI	dyne	DYN
drop	GT	dysprosium	DY
drug	APC; AZT; BST; DEX; E; GHB; H; HCG; LSD; MDMA; NSAID; PAS; PCP; PH; POT; Q; SSRI; TAB		

each	EA; PER	Economic and Social Committee	ESC
each month	PCM	Economic Commission for Europe	ECE
each thousand	PERMIL		
each week	PW		
each year	PA; PERAN	economic development council	NEDC;
earl	E		
early	AM	economical; economics	ECON
early English	EE		
Early English Text Society	EETS	economist	MECON
		economy	ECON
early hours	AM	ecstasy	E; MDMA
earned run average	ERA	Ecuador	EC
earnings per share	EPS	eczema society	NES
earth	E	Edgar	ED; NED
east	E	Edinburgh	EDIN; EH
East Africa	EA	edited	ED; EDIT
East Anglia	EA	Edith	EDY
East Caribbean	EC	edition	AUFL; ED; EDIT
east central	EC	editor	ED; EDIT
East End	EC	editorial assistant	SUB
East Germany	DDR	Edmund	ED; NED
East Indian; East Indies	EI	educated; education	ED
		educated man	BA; MA; *see also* Appendix: Degrees
eastern	E		
Eastern European Time	EET	education and achievement details	CV
Eastern Standard Time	EST	education department	SED
Eastern Time	ET	Educational Institute of Scotland	EIS
east-north-east	ENE		
east-south-east	ESE	educational paper	TES
eccentricity	E	educational researchers	NFER
Ecclesiastes	ECCL; ECCLES	educationalist	BED; DED; MED
ecclesiastical	ECCL; ECCLES	educationally subnormal	ESN
Ecclesiasticus	ECCLUS; SIR		
echo	E	Edward	E; ED; NED; TED
ecological; ecology	ECOL	Edward, King and Emperor	ERI
economic	ECON	Edwin	ED; NED
Economic and Monetary Union	EMU	effects	FX
		egg	O

ego	I	electromagnetic interference	EMI
Egypt	ET; UAR	electromagnetic unit	EMU
eight	VIII	electromotive force	E; EMF
eighty	LXXX; R	electromyogram; electromyograph	EMG
eighty thousand	R		
einsteinium	ES	electron	E
Eisenhower	IKE	electron microscope	SEM; TEM
el	L	electron spectroscopy	ESCA
El Salvador	ES	electron spin resonance	ESR
elder	OAP; SNR; SR		
electoral system	PR	electronic	E
electric	ELEC; ELECT	electronic charge	E
electric charge	Q	electronic countermeasures	ECM
electric current	AC; DC; I		
electric field strength	E	electronic data interchange	EDI
electric flux	D		
electric multiple unit	EMU	electronic data processing	EDP
electric shock treatment	EST	electronic funds transfer	EFT
electrical	LX	electronic intelligence	ELINT
electrical capacitance	C	electronic news gathering	ENG
electrical manufacturer	EKCO		
electrical skin resistance	ESR	electronic number plate	ENP
electrical stimulation of the brain	ESB	electronic point of sale	EPOS
		electronic serial number	ESN
electricals	LX		
electricity	ELEC; ELECT; HT	electronics	ICE
electricity regulator's office	OFFER	electronvolt(s)	EV
		electroplated	EP
electrocardiogram; electrocardiograph	ECG	electro-selective pattern	ESP
electroconvulsive therapy	ECT	electrostatic document analysis	ESDA
electroencephalogram; electroencephalograph	EEG	electrostatic precipitator	ESP
electro-explosive device	EED	electrostatic unit	ESU
electromagnetic field	EMF		
electromagnetic force	EMF		

full form	abbreviation	full form	abbreviation
element	*see* Appendix: Chemical Elements	end of year	DEC
		End Physical Punishment of Children	EPOCH
elevated railroad	EL; L		
eleven	11; O; XI	endogenous retroviruses	ERV
eleven thousand	O		
Eliot	TS	endorse	OK
élite	A1	endorsement	OK
Elizabeth	BET; E; ER; LIZ	energy	E
Ely: of Ely	ELIEN	energy foundation	NEF
em	M	Energy Technology Support Unit	ETSU
embryo transfer	ET		
emcee	MC	engine	ATP
emergency detection system	SARSAT	engineer	BAI; BE; BENG; CE; CENG; CHE; DENG; DING; ENG; ME; RE
Emergency Medical Service	EMS		
emergency room	ER	engineering	ENG
eminence	VIP	Engineering and Technology Board	ETB
Eminent Persons' Group	EPG	Engineering Council UK	ECUK
Emma	EM; EMM	Engineering Employers' Federation	EEF
emotional and behavioural difficulties; emotional and behavioural disorder	EBD	engineering laboratory	NEL
		engineers	AEEU; EMA; ICE; ICHEME; IEE; IMECHE; IMINE; ME; RE; REME; SAE; SE
emperor	EMP; IMP		
emphysema	COPD	England	ENG
empire	EMP	England and Wales Cricket Board	ECB
employment trainee	ET		
employment training	ET	English	E; ENG
empress	EMP; IMP	English as a foreign language	EFL
en	N		
en passant	EP	English as a second language	ESL
enclosed; enclosure	ENC; ENCL		
encyclopaedia; encyclopaedic	ENCY; ENCYC; ENCYCL	English Dialect Society	EDS
		English for academic purposes	EAP
end of tape	EOT		
end of transmission	EOT		

full form ⇨ abbreviation

English for speakers of other languages	ESOL	environmental protection technology	EPT
English for specific purposes	ESP	environmentalist	EHO
		environmentalists	ACRE; EA; EEA; EPA; FOE
English Golf Union	EGU		
English language teaching	ELT	environmentally sensitive area	ESA
English National Opera	ENO	envoy extraordinary	ENVEXT
		enzyme	ADA
English person	POM	ephemeris time	ET
English Tourism Council	ETC	Ephesians	EPH
		epigraph	RIP
English Tourist Board	ETB	Epiphany	EPIPH
English Version	EV	epiphenomenon	ESP
English, Welsh and Scottish Railway	EWS	Episcopal	EPIS
		Episcopalian	PE
English-Speaking Union	ESU	epistle	EP; EPIS
engraver; engraving	ENG	epitaph	RIP
enhanced graphic adapter	EGA	Epstein-Barr	EB
		Epstein-Barr virus	EBV
enhanced messaging service	EMS	equal	EQ
enhanced radiation weapon	ERW	Equal Opportunities Commission	EOC
Enigmatic Variations	EV	Equal Rights Amendment	ERA
enlarged	AUGM	equation	EQ
Enrolled Nurse	EN; ENG	equivalent	EQ
ensign	ENS	equivalent grade	EG
enterprise	SME	erbium	ER
Enterprise Investment Scheme	EIS	erected this monument	HMP
Enterprise Zone Trust	EZT	errors excepted	EE
entertainers	CSE; ENSA	erstwhile	EX
entomology	ENT	escape	ESC
entropy	S	escudo	ESC
environment agency	EA	Esdras	ESD
environmental health officer	EHO	especially	ESP; ESPEC
		esquire	ESQ; ESQR
environmental impact assessment	EIA	essential fatty acid	EFA

Full form	Abbreviation	Full form	Abbreviation
established	EST	ex	X
Established Church	EC	ex dividend	EXDIV; XD
estate	EST	ex libris	EXLIB
Esther	ESTH	ex officio	EO; EXOFF
estimate	E	ex works	EXW
estimated	EST	exact; exactly	TOAT
estimated time of arrival	ETA	exam; examination	A; AS; CSE; EX; GCE; GCSE; HNC; O; ONC; SC; SCE
Estonia	EST		
estuary	EST		
et cetera; et ceteri	ETC	examination board	OCR
Ethiopia	ETH	examined	EX
ethyl	ET	examiners	ABRSM
ethylene dichloride	EDC	example	EX
etymological; etymology	ETY; ETYM; ETYMOL	excellency	EXC
		excellent	A1; EXC; FAB
EU policy	CAP	except	EX; EXC
Eugenia; Eugenie	ENA	except as otherwise noted	EAON
euphemism; euphemistically	EUPH	excepted	EX
		exception	EX; EXC
euro	EUR	excessive; excessively	OTT
Europe	EUR	exchange	EX; EXCH; PABX; PAX; PBX
European	E; EUR		
European Anti-Fraud Office	OLAF	exchange rate mechanism	ERM
European Commission	EC	exchequer	EXCH
European Community	EC	exclamation	EXCL
European Monetary Union	EMU	excluding	EXCL
		exclusive	EXCL
European Union	EU	exclusive economic zone	EEZ
europium	EU		
evangelical	EVAN; EVANG; SIM	excursion	EX; EXC
		excursus	EX
Evangelical Union	EU	executed	EX
even	EEN	executive	EX; EXEC
evenings	EVGS	executive committee	EC
ever	EER	executive officer	CEO; EO; SEO
every other day	EOD	executor	EXEC; EXOR; EXR
evolutionarily stable strategy	ESS		

full form ⇨ abbreviation

full form	abbreviation	full form	abbreviation
executrix	EXRX	extensible mark-up language	XML
exercise; exercises	PE; PT	extension	EXT
Exeter	EXON	exterior	EXT
Exeter: of Exeter	EXON	external; externally	EXT
exhibition centre	NEC	extinct	EXT
Exodus	EX; EXOD	extra	EX; EXT; LB; NB; W; X
expanded memory system	EMS	extra extra large	XXL
expendable launch vehicle	ELV	extra large	OS; XL
experiment; experimental	EXP	extra low frequency	ELF
expert	PRO	extract	EXT
expired	EXP	extrasensory perception	ESP
expiry	EXP	extraterrestrial	ET
explosive	ANFO; HE; RDX; TNT	extravehicular activity	EVA
explosives	HE	extreme pressure	EP
exponential	EXP	extremely high frequency	EHF
export	EX; EXP	extremely low frequency	ELF
express	EX; EXP	eye	PI; TEC
ex-serviceman	VET	Ezekiel	EZEK
extempore; extemporize	ADLIB	Ezra	EZ
extended memory section	XMS		

F

facsimile	FAX	Federation Against Software Theft	FAST
Faculty of Actuaries	FA	Federation of German Industries	BDI
Fahrenheit	F		
fair	OK	feet	F; FT
fair average quality	FAQ	feet per second	FPS
fair trading office	OFT	fellow	BRO; F; M
fairly quiet; fairly soft	MP	fellows	FF
fall	OCT	female	F
familiar	FAM	feminine	F; FEM
family	FAM	femtometre(s)	FM
Family Income Supplement	FIS	fermium	FM
Family Planning Association	FPA	fertility treatment	AI; AID; AIH; DI; GIFT; ICSI; IVF; ZIFT
Fanny Adams	FA	fertilization	AID; AIH; DI; ICSI; IVF
fantastic	FAB	fever	Q
farad	F	few	I; II; III; IV; IX; V; VI; VII; VIII; X
faraday	F	field marshal	FM
Faraday's constant	F	field officer	FO
farewell	BV; BYE	field-effect transistor	FET
farmers	NFU	fifteen	XV
Faroe Islands	FO	fifty	A; L
farthing	F	fifty thousand	L
fascists	BNP; NF	fighter; fighter aircraft	EFA; F; MIG; MRCA
fashionable	IN; U	figurative; figuratively	FIG
fast forward	FF	figure	FIG; I; V; X
fast-breed reactor	FBR	Fiji	FJI
fat	OS	file allocation table	FAT
father	DA; DAD; FR; PA; POP; REV	file format	DOC; EPS; GIF; HTM; HTML; JPEG; JPG; PDF; PNG; PS; RTF; TIF; TIFF; TXT
father of the chapel	FOC		
fathom	F; FM; FTH; FTHM		
fathoms	F	filial generation	F
February	FEB	film	CEL; ET; PIC
federal	FED	film classification	A; AA; G; PG; R; U; X
Federation Against Copyright Theft	FACT		

film speed	ISO	flatter squarer tube	FST
film studio	MGM; RKO	flavour enhancer	MSG
film theatre	NFT	fleet	*see* navy
final	Z	Fleet Air Arm	FAA
final character;	Z	flier	*see* airman
final letter		fliers	*see* airmen
financial advisers	AIFA	floor	FL; KO
financial officer	CFO	Flora	FLO
Financial Times	FT	Florence	FLO
Financial Times Index	FTSE	Florida	FA; FL; FLA;
fine	A1; F; OK		FLOR
Finland	FIN	florin	FL; FLOR
Finnish	FINN	floruit	FL
fire extinguisher	BCF	flourished	FL; FLOR
fire officer	CFO	flower	MUM; R
fire service	NFS	fluid	FL
fireplug	FP; H	fluid ounce(s)	FLOZ
firm	*see* company	fluorine	F
first	A; 1; 1ST; NO1	flux	D
first character	A	flying bomb	V1
first class	A; A1; EXC	flying officer	FO
First Division	FDA	flying saucer	UFO
Association		fly-killer	DDT
first in, first out	FIFO	foetal alcohol	FAS
first in, last out	FILO	syndrome	
first letter	A	Fog Intensive	FIDO
first-rate	A; A1; EXC	Dispersal Operation	
first-timer	DEB	folio	F; FO; FOL
first-year allowance	FYA	folios	FF
fit	A1	followed	FOL
five	V	following	F; FF; FOL; SEQ;
five hundred	A; D; Q		SQ
five hundred thousand	Q	fool	BF
five shillings	CR	foot	F; FT
five thousand	A	football	*see* rugby
fivepence	VD; VP	Football Association	FA
flak	AA	football club	AFC; FC; QPR
flash	MO; S; SEC	football league	NFL
flatten	KO	football team	11; QPR; XI

footballers	AFA; FA; PFA; SFA	forum	BBS
footnote	PS	forward	FWD
foot-pound-second	FPS	forzando	FZ
footwear	DMS	four	IV
for all to see	U	four hundred	G; P
for and on behalf of	PP	four hundred thousand	G; P
for example; for instance	EG; ZB	four times a day	QID
		fourth-rate	D
for the attention of	ATTN; FAO	four-wheel drive	FWD
for the meantime	ADINT	foxhunter	MFH
for the time being	PROTEM	foxtrot	F
for your information	FYI	fragment	FR
force	BEF; E; F; G; OGPU; RAF; RN; SS; TA	frames per second	FPS
		franc(s)	F; FF; FR
		France	F; FR
forced	FZ; SF	Franciscan(s)	OFM; OSF
forces' chaplain	CF; HCF; OCF	francium	FR
forces' entertainers	CSE; ENSA	fraternity	FRAT
foreign exchange	FOREX	fraternize	FRAT
Foreign Office	FO	free	NC; WC
Forensic Science Service	FSS	free alongside quay	FAQ
		free alongside ship	FAS
Forestry Commission	FC	Free Church	FC
fork	Y	Free Democratic Republic	FDR
form feed	FF		
former	EX	free of charge	FOC
former drinkers	AA	free on board	FOB
former partner	EX	free on rail	FOR
former pupil	FP; OB	Free Presbyterian	FP
former spouse	EX	free trade agreement	FTA
fort	FT	freezing point	FP
forte	F	Freight Transport Association	FTA
fortepiano	FP		
fortissimo	FF	French	FR
fortississimo	FFF	French African Colonies	CFA
forty	F; XL		
forty thousand	F	French company	CIE; SA
forty-nine	IL	French franc(s)	FF
		French lawyer	AV

full form ⇨ abbreviation

French Pacific Banks	CFP	from the sign	DS
French Pacific Colonies	CFP	front-wheel drive	FWD
French Republic	RF	fuel	LNG; LPG; LRP; RDF; SURF
French TV broadcasting system	SECAM	full organ	FO
Frenchman	M	full service history	FSH
Frenchmen	MM	full-time	FT
Frenchwoman	MLLE; MME	function; function of an angle	COS; COSEC; COSECH; COSH; COT; COTH; COVERS; SEC; SECH; SIN; SINH; TAN; TANH
frequency	F		
frequency modulation	FM		
frequently	FR		
frequently asked questions	FAQ		
		fund	ABF; IMF; SCF; UNICEF
friar	DOM; FR; OP		
friars	*see* monk(s)	fungicide	PCP; TBT
Friday	FR; FRI	furlong	F; FUR
from	EX	furlongs	F
from the beginning	ABINIT	further education	FE
from the books of	EXLIB	future	FUT
from the founding of the city	AUC	futures exchange	LIFFE

Gabon	G	General Assembly	GA
gadolinium	GD	general average	GA
Gaelic	GAEL	General Electric	GE
Gaelic developer	CNAG	general headquarters	GHQ
Galatians	GAL	general information	GEN
gallium	GA	general intelligence	G
gallon	CONG; G; GAL; GALL	general issue	GI
		general manager	GM
gallons	G; GAL; GALL	General Motors	GM
Gallup Poll	GP	General Post Office	GPO
The Gambia	WAG	general practitioner	GP
game	RL; RU	general practitioners	RCGP
games	PE; PT	general secretary	GS
gangster	AL	general staff	GS
gaol	PEN	general staff officer	GSO
gardeners	RHS	Genesis	GEN
gardens	GDNS	genetic disorder	MFS
Garry; Gary	GAZ	genetically modified	GM
gas	AR; CFC; CL; CO; CS; F; H; HE; HFC; KR; LNG; LPG; N; NE; NOX; O; RN; SNG; XE	genetically modified organism	GMO
		genitive	GEN
		gent; gentleman	ESQ; MR
gas constant	R	gentlemen	MESSRS; MM; *see also* toilet
gas installers	CORGI		
gauss	G; GS	gently	DOL
gave and dedicated as a gift	DDD	gents	LAT; LAV; LOO; WC
		geographers	RGS
gave as a gift	DD	geographic; geographical; geography	GEOG
gave to God	DD		
gazette; gazetteer	GAZ		
gazunder	PO	geologic; geological; geology	GEOL
gee	G		
gee-gee	GG	George	G; GEO; GR
Geiger-Müller; Geiger-Müller counter	GM	George Cross	GC
		George, King and Emperor	GRI
gelatine	GEL		
general	CINC; GEN; GENL; GOC; IKE	George Medal	GM
		Georgia	GA; GE
		German	G; GER
		German company	AG; GMBH

German Democratic Republic	DDR; GDR	good clinical practice	GCP
German troops	SS	good man; good person	S; ST
Germanic	GMC	good sense of humour	GSOH
germanium	GE	good woman	S; ST; STE
Germany	D; FRG; GER	goods and services tax	GST
germicide	TCP	Gotham	NY
gerund; gerundive	GER	gourde	G; GDE
Ghana	GH	government	G; GOV; HMG
GI	JOE	government issue	GI
Gibraltar	GBZ; GIB	government think-tank	CPRS
gigabyte(s)	GB	governor	GOV; HE; *see also* dad
giga-electronvolt(s)	GEV	Grace	DR; WG
gigahertz	GHZ	grade point average	GPA
gigawatt(s)	GW	gradually slowing	RALL; RIT
gilbert	GB; GIL	graduate	BA; MA; *see also* Appendix: Degrees
Gilbert and Sullivan	GANDS	graduated pension	GP
gin and tonic	GANDT	Gräfenberg	G
girder	RSJ	graft-versus-host	GVH
girl	DEB; G; SIS; *see also* Appendix: First Names	grain	GR
		gram(s); gramme(s)	G; GM; GR
gives, devotes and dedicates	DDD	grammar school	GS
Gladstone	GOM	grams per square metre; grammes per square metre	GSM
glamour	SA		
glasses	OO	gran turismo	GT
glory to the Father	GP	gran turismo injection	GTI
Gloucestershire	GLOS	grand	G; K; M
G-men	FBI	Grand Cross of Hanover	GCH
God	D; DOM	grand master	GM
God willing	DV	grand old man	GOM
gold	AU	Grand Old Party	GOP
golden arches	M	Grand Prix	GP
golf	G	Grand Unified Theory	GUT
golfers	EGU; LGU; PGA; USGA	grandmother	NAN
gong	*see* Appendix: Decorations	grant	FIS
		grant-maintained	GM
good	G; PI		

graphic interchange format	GIF	group	GP; *see also* company
graphical user interface	GUI	group of	G
gratis	WC	grove	GRO
gravity	G	growth hormone	GH
gray	GY	guaranteed	GTD
great	FAB; G; GT; OS	guards	CG; RGG; RHG
Great Britain	GB; UK	Guatemala	GCA
great number	C; D; K; M	Guernsey	GBG
great sense of humour	GSOH	guest	PG
greatest	MAX	guilder	GLD
greatest common measure	GCM	guinea	LS; RG
Greece	GR	guineas	GS
Greek	GK; GR	gumshoe	*see* detective
Greek Cypriot unionists	EOKA	gun	*see* weapon
green	ECO	gunner	RA
Grenada	WG	guns	HA
grey	GR	gutta	GT
grievous bodily harm	GBH	Guyana	GUY
gross	GR	gym	PE; PT
ground control apparatus	GCA	gymnasium	GYM
ground-launched cruise missile	GLCM	gymnastic	GYM
		gymnastics	GYM; PE; PT

Habakkuk	HAB	he/she made	FEC
had	D	he/she painted	PINX
haemoglobin	HB	he/she sculpted	SC; SCULP; SCULPT
haemorrhage	CVA	head(s)	*see* toilet
hafnium	HF	Head Office	HO
Haggai	HAG	head teachers	NAHT
hahnium	HA	headquarters	HQ
Hail Mary	AM	head-up display	HUD
hairpin	U	healer	DR; GP; MD
hairstyle	DA	health service	NHS
Haiti	RH	heaps	C; D; K; L; M
half	HF	hearts	H
half century	L	heater	RAD
half day	AM; PM	Heath	TED
half pay	HP	heating system	CH
half-a-dozen	VI	Heavy Artillery	HA
half-time	HT	heavy goods vehicle	HGV
Hampshire	HANTS	heavy-duty	HD
hand	H; L; R	Hebrew; Hebrews	HEB; HEBR
handful	V	hectare(s)	HA
handicap	HCP	hectogram(s)	HG
hands	HH	hectolitre(s)	HL
handwriting	MS	hectometre(s)	HM
hangover	DT; DTS	height	H; HT
Hannah	HAN; NAN	heir	HER
harbourmaster	HM	helium	HE
hard	H	help	SOS
hard black	HB	henry	H; HAL; HY; O
has	S	Her Grace	HG
hassium	HS	Her Highness	HH
hast	ST	Her Imperial Majesty	HIM
have	HA; VE	Her Majesty; Her Majesty's	HM
Hawaii	HI		
Hawaii Standard Time	HST	heraldry	HER
Hawaiian Islands	HI	Herbert	AP; APH
he/she designed	INV	here	AHL
he/she devised	INV	hermit friar(s)	OSA
he/she drew	DEL		

hero	*see* Appendix: Decorations	His Imperial Majesty	HIM
heroin	H	His Majesty; His Majesty's	HM
Hertfordshire	HERTS		
hertz	CS; H; HZ	histology	HIST
Hester	HETTY	historian	HIST
heterosexual	HET	historians	RHS
hexadecimal	HEX	history	HIST
high class	U	Hitler's bodyguard	SS
high explosive	HE; TNT	holiday	HOL; VAC
high frequency	HF	holidays	HOLS
High German	HG	Holland	*see* The Netherlands
high memory area	HMA		
high note	ELA	holmium	HO
high pressure	HP	holograph	MS
high priest	HP	holy	PI
high school	HS	holy books	NT; OT
high tension	HT	Holy Communion	HC
high voltage	HV	holy man	S; ST
high water mark	HWM	Holy Mother Mary	SMM
high-class	A; A1; U	Holy Roman Emperor; Holy Roman Empire	HRE
high-definition television	HDTV		
		Holy See	V
high-density lipoprotein	HDL	Holy Virgin	SV
		holy woman	S; ST; STE
highest common factor	HCF	home counties	SE
		Home Guard	LDV
highest note	ELA	Home Office	HO
Highland and Islands Enterprise	HIE	home rule	HR
		Home Secretary	HS
high-speed train	HST; TGV	homework	DIY
Hindu nationalists	BJP	Honduras	HN
Hindustani	HIND	honey	HON; SIS
hire purchase	HP	Hong Kong	HK
His Eminence	HE	honorary	HON
His Excellency	HE	Honour	A; CB; CBE; CH; 10; J; K; MBE; OBE; OM; Q; *see also* Appendix: Decorations
His Grace	HG		
His Highness	HH		
His Holiness	HH		

Honourable	HON	hug	O
honourable companion	CH	huge	OS
		hum	BO
hoop	O	Human Genome Organisation	HUGO
hopper	ROO		
hormone	ACTH; ADH; EPO; FSH; HGH; ICSH; LH	human growth hormone	HGH
		human resources	HR
horse	GG; H; PAD	humourless	PO
horse artillery	RHA	hundred	C; CENT
horsepower	CV; HP; PS	hundred and fifty	CL; Y
horticulturalists	RHS	hundred and fifty thousand	Y
Hosea	HOS		
hospital	BARTS; GOSH; H; MASH; QMC; SAN; UCH	hundred and sixty	T
		hundred and sixty thousand	T
hospital bug	MRSA	hundred dollars	C
hospital department	CCU; ECG; ENT; ICU; MRI; OT; REHAB; SCBU	hundred thousand	C
		hundredweight(s)	CWT
		Hungarian	HUNG
host	MC	Hungary	H; HUNG
hostage	POW	hurrah	RAH
hostel	Y; YHA	husband	H
hostilities only	HO	hustler	PRO
hot	H	hydrant	FP; H
hot and cold	HANDC	hydrogen	H
hotel	H	hyperbaric oxygen	HBO
hour	H; HR	hyperbolic cosecant	COSECH
house	H; HC; HK; HL; HO; HR; HSE	hyperbolic cosine	COSH
		hyperbolic cotangent	COTH
House of Commons	HC	hyperbolic secant	SECH
House of Keys	HK	hyperbolic sine	SINH
House of Lords	HL	hyperbolic tangent	TANH
House of Representatives	HR	hypotenuse	HYP
Houses of Parliament	HP	hypothesis	HYP
housework	DIY	hypothetical	HYP

I	A; J	imperial gallon(s)	IMPGAL; IMPGALL
I am	IM	impersonal	IMPERS
I had	ID	implant	*see* fertility treatment
I have	IVE	impromptu	ADLIB
I should	ID	in	I
Iceland	IS	in charge	IC
id est	DH; IE; SC	in command	IC
Idaho	ID; IDA	in connection with	RE
ideal	A1	in English	ANG
identification; identity	ID	in equal quantities of each	A; AA
ie	DH; SC	in its place	INLOC
illicit diamond buying	IDB	in my humble opinion	IMHO
Illinois	IL; ILL	in my opinion	IMO
illiterate	ILLIT	in other words	SC; SCIL; SCIZ
illness	AD; ADD; ADHD; AIDS; ALD; ALS; ARD; BSE; CFS; CHD; CJD; COPD; CWD; DI; DM; DMD; DS; EB; FLU; FMD; GPI; GVHD; HIV; IBS; KS; ME; MND; MS; NSU; NVCJD; OCD; PCP; PID; PKU; PMDD; PND; PTSD; RA; RP; SAD; SARS; STD; TB; TSE; URI; VD	in the absence of the accused	ABSERE; ABSRE
		in the afternoon	PM
		in the last month	ULT
		in the meantime	ADINT
		in the modern age	AD
		in the morning	AM
		in the name of God	IND
		in the place cited	LC
		in the place of the seal	LS
		in the same place	IB; IBID
illustrated	ILL	in the time of	TEMP
illustration	EG	in the work cited	OPCIT
imaginary number	I	in the year	A; AN
image building	PR	in the year from the building of the city	AUC
imitation; imitative	IMIT	in the year of Hegira	AH
immediately	STAT	in the year of human salvation	AHS
impedance	Z	in the year of our Lord	AD
imperative	IMPER	in the year of salvation	AS
imperfect	IMPERF	in the year of the King's reign	ARR
imperial	IMP		

in the year of the Lord	AD	infection	AIDS; BSE; CJD; FLU; FMD; HIV; NSU; NVCJD; PCP; PID; SARS; STD; TB; URI; VD
in the year of the Queen's reign	ARR		
in the year of the world	AM		
in this sense	HS	infectious diseases	ID
in this year	HA	inferior	INF
inboard	INBD	infertility treatment	*see* fertility treatment
inch	IN		
inches	IN; INS	infinite	N
including; inclusive	INC; INCL	infinitive	INF; INFIN
income support	FIS; IS	inflation measure	CPI; RPI
incorporated	INC	influenced	INFL
indefinite	INDEF	influenza	FLU
indefinite number	N	informal	INF
independence	I	information	GEN; I; INF
independent	I; IND	information and communication technology	ICT
independent financial adviser	IFA		
independent suspension	IS	information department	ID
index	CPI; FTSE; NNI; RPI; TPI	information science	IS
		information systems	IS
India	I; IND	information technology	ADP; IT
Indian	IND		
Indiana	IN; IND	infrared	IR
indicated air speed	IAS	inheritance tax	IHT
indicative	INDIC	initial public offering	IPO
indium	IN	initial teaching alphabet	ITA
individual	INDIV		
individual savings account	ISA	injury	ABH; GBH; NAI; RSI
Indo-European	IE	Inland Revenue	IR
Indo-Germanic	IG	inn	PH
Indonesia	RI	inner diameter	ID
inductance	L	innumerable	N
inevitable; inevitably	TINA	input/output	IO
inexperienced driver	L	insecticide	BHC; BT; DDT; OP
infantry	INF		

in-service education and training	INSET	interest	APR; INT
inspectors	ETI	interference device	SQUID
instant	INST; MO; S; SEC	intergovernmental conference	IGC
institute	I; INST	interior	INT
institute for deaf people	RNID	interjection	INTERJ
institute for blind people	RNIB	intermediate frequency	IF
Institute of Contemporary Arts	ICA	internal	INT
		internal combustion	IC
institution	INST	internal combustion engine	ICE
instruction	RI	internal security	IS
instrument	*see* musical instrument	international	I; INT
instrument approach system	IAS	International Atomic Time	TAI
instrument flying regulations	IFR	International Automobile Federation	FIA
instrument flying rules	IFR	International Cycling Union	UCI
instrument landing system	ILS	International Equestrian Federation	FEI
insurance	INS	International Football Federation	FIFA
insurer	ACII		
insurers	ABI; BUPA; CII; PRU	International Gymnastics Federation	FIG
integrated circuit	IC	International Monetary Fund	IMF
integrated data processing	IDP	International Olympic Committee	IOC
integrated development environment	IDE	international phonetic alphabet	IPA
integrated drive electronics	IDE	International Road Transport	TIR
intelligence	CIA; GEN; GRU; IQ; MI	International Ski Federation	FIS
		international system	SI
intelligence department	ID	international unit	IU
intelligence quotient	IQ	Internet connection	DSL
intelligence service	CIA; GRU	Internet Protocol	IP
intelligent character recognition	ICR	Internet service	BIDS

Internet service provider	AOL; ISP; WISP	irregularly	IRREG
		is	S
Internet system	BIDS	Isaac	IK; IKE; IKY
intradermal	ID	Isabel; Isabella; Isbel; Ishbel; Isobel	BEL; IB; ISA; TIB
intrauterine	IU		
intravenous	IV	Isaiah	IS; ISA
intravenous drip	IV	Isbel; Ishbel	*see* Isabel
intravenously	IV	island	I; IOM; IOW; IS; ISL; IW
intuition	ESP		
Invalid Care Allowance	ICA	islands	IS
		isle	I; IOM; IOW; IS; IW
invasion day	DDAY		
invented	INV	Isle of Man	GBM; IOM
investigators	CIB; CID; FBI	Isle of Wight	IOW; IW
invoice	INV	isles	IS
iodine	I	Isobel	*see* Isabel
IOU	PN	isolated replay	ISO
Iowa	IA	Israel	IL
Iran	IR	it	SA; T
Iraq	IRQ	it is not permitted	NL
Ireland	IR; IRL	it is not clear	NL
iridium	IR	Italian	IT; ITAL
Irish	IR	Italian vermouth	IT
Irish Free State	IFS	italic	ITAL
Irish Radio and Television	RTE	Italy	I; IT; ITAL
		Ivor	IVY
iron	FE	Ivory Coast	CI
irregular	IRREG; TA	izzard	Z

J

jack	J; *see also* sailor	Joint European Torus	JET
jacket	DJ; TUX	joint stock company	AG
jail	PEN	joist	RSJ
jake	OK	jollies; jolly	RM
Jamaica	JA; JAM	Jonah	JON
James	JAS; JIM	Jonathan; Jonathon	JON
Janet	JAN	Jordan	HKJ
Janice	JAN	Joseph	JO; JOE; JOS
jankers	KP	Josepha; Josephine	JO; JOE
jansky	JY	Joshua	JOSH
January	JAN	joule	J
Japan	J	journal	FT; J; TES; TLS
Japanese	JAP	journalist	ED; FJI; MCIJ; SUB
Jay	J	journalists	CIOJ; IOJ; NUJ
Jenifer; Jennifer	JEN	judge	CHJ; CJ; J; JP; LCJ; LJ; REF; UMP
Jeremiah	JER		
jerks	GYM; PE; PT		
jerry	PO	judges	JJ; JUD; JUDG
Jersey	GBJ	Judith	JUD
Jesuit(s)	SJ	Juliet	J
Jesus Christ	IHC; IHS; INRI; JC	Julius Caesar	JC
		July	JUL; JY
jet	*see* fighter	jumbo	OS
jiffy	MO; S; SEC	jumper	ROO
jitters	DT; DTS	junction	T
Joanna	JO	June	JUN
Jobseeker's Allowance	JSA	junior	JNR; JR; JUN; JUNR
Jock	DJ; MAC		
Joe	GI	justice	CHJ; J; JP
joey	ROO	Justice of the Peace	JP
john	*see* toilet	justices	JJ
joint	J	just-in-time	JIT
Joint Chiefs of Staff	JCS	juvenile	JUV

kalium	K	kilohertz	KHZ
Kansas	KAN; KANS; KS	kilojoule(s)	KJ
kaon	K	kilolitre(s)	KL
karat	K; KT	kilometre(s)	K; KM
katal	KAT	kilometres per gallon	KPG
Katharine; Katherine	KAY; KIT	kilometres per hour	KMH; KPH
Kay	K	kiloton(s); kilotonne(s)	KT
Kazakhstan	KZ	kilovolt(s)	KV
keep	RET	kilowatt(s)	KW
keg(s)	KG	kilowatt-hour(s)	KWH
kelvin	K	Kimball	KIM
Kennel Club	KC	Kimberley	KIM
Kenneth	KEN	kina	K
Kent	SE	kinetic energy	KE
Kentucky	KEN; KY	king	CR, ER; ERI; GR;
Kenya	EAK		GRI; HM; K; R
Kevin	KEV	King and Emperor	RI
key	A; B; C; D; E;	King Charles	CR
	ESC; F; G	King Edward	ER
keyword and context	KWAC	King George	GR
keyword in context	KWIC	King's Bench	KB
keyword out of context	KWOC	King's Counsel	KC
kick-off	KO	king's son	P
killer	ALCM; ASM;	Kirkpatrick	K
	BHC; BT; DDT;	kiss	X
	GAT; ICBM;	kitchen police	KP
	MRBM; NK; OP;	Kiwi	NZ
	PCP; SAM; SSM;	knave	J
	STEN; TASM;	knight	AK; K; KB; KBE;
	TBT; *see also*		KCB; KCMG;
	weapon		KCVO; KG; KM;
kilo	K		KP; KSTJ; KT; N
kilobyte	K; KB; KBYTE	knight bachelor	KB
kilobytes	K; KB; KBYTES	Knight of Australia	AK
kilocalorie(s)	C; CAL; KCAL	Knight of the Garter	KG
kilocycle(s)	KC	Knight of the Thistle	KT
kilo-electronvolt(s)	KEV	knit	K
kilogram(s);	KG	knock out	KO
kilogramme(s)		knocked down	KD
kilogray(s)	KGY		

full form ⇨ abbreviation

knockout	KO	krone	K; KR
knot	KN; KT	krypton	KR
knots	KN	Kuala Lumpur	KL
Köchel	K	kurchatovium	KU
Korea	PRK; ROK	Kuwait	KWT
koruna	KC	Kuwaiti dinar	KD
Kosovo Force	KFOR	kwacha	K
krona	K; KR	Kyrgyzstan	KS
króna	K; KR		

laboratory	LAB
labour	LAB
Labour Party	LP
Labrador	LAB
lad	*see* Appendix: First Names
ladies	*see* toilet
Lady Day	LD
Lady Literate in Arts	LLA
Lady Provost	LP
laevorotatory	L
lag	CON
lake	L
lambert	L
lamentations	LAM
Lancashire	LANCS
land measure	A
lane	LA
language	APL; ASL; COL; HTML; IAL; JCL; LANG; NF; OE; OF; PDL; PL; QL; RPG; SANS; SANSK; SGML; SKR; SKT; SQL; VRML; WML; XML
lanthanum	LA
Laos	LAO
large	L; LG; LGE; OS
large goods vehicle	LGV
large number	C; CD; D; K; L; M
large-scale integration	LSI
lass	*see* Appendix: First Names
last	ULT; Z
last character	Z
last in, first out	LIFO
last in, last out	LILO
last letter	Z
last month	DEC; ULT
late	D; EX
Late Latin	LL
lateral	LAT
latest	GEN
Latin	L; LAT
latissimus dorsi	LAT
latitude	L; LAT
Latter-Day Saints	LDS
Latvia	LV
lavatory	*see* toilet
lawmaker	MEP; MP
lawmakers	LA; LEG
lawman	*see* lawyer
Lawn Tennis Association	LTA
Lawrence	DH; TE
lawrencium	LR; LW
lawyer	AV; BCL; BL; DA; DCL; KC; QC
layer	E
lead	PB
leader	CO; ED; PM
leader writer	ED
leading	LDG
leading aircraftman; leading aircraftsman	LAC
leading aircraftswoman; leading aircraftwoman	LACW
leaf	F; P
league	L
learner	L
least common denominator	LCD
least common multiple	LCM
leatherneck	RM
leaves	FF; PP

full form ⇨ abbreviation

Lebanon	RL	level	A; O
lecture	LECT	leveraged buyout	LBO
lecturer	L; LECT	Leviticus	LEV; LEVIT
left	L; VO	Lewis	LEW
left centre	LC	lexicon	LEX; OED; TCD
left hand	LH	liberal	L; LIB
left-footer	RC	liberation	LIB
left-hand drive	LHD	liberationists	ALF; PFLP; PLO
left-hand page	VO	Liberia	LB
leg before	LB	libra	L
leg before wicket	LBW	librarian	ALA; LIB
leg bye	LB	library	BL; DLL; LC; LIB; PL; RL
legal	LEG		
legate	LEG	Library Association	LA
legato	LEG	Library of Congress	LC
legislation; legislative	LEG; LEGIS	Libya	LAR; LY
legislative assembly	LA	licentiate	L
legislator	MEP; MP	Liechtenstein	FL
legislators	HP; LA; LEG	lieutenant	DL; LIEUT; LT; LVO; NO1; SUB
legislature	LEG; LEGIS		
Leicestershire	LEICS	life; life story	BIO; CV
Leipzig	LEIP	lifeboat institution	RNLI
length	L; LGTH	ligament	ACL
Leonard	LEN	light	UV
Leslie	LES	light infantry	LI
Lesotho	LS	light-emitting diode	LED
less developed country	LDC	lighting technicians	LX
let a mixture be made	MFT	light-water reactor	LWR
let her/him take	CAP	lightweight	OZ
lethal dosage	LD	light-year(s)	LY
letter	COL; COLOSS; EP; EPH; EPIS; GAL; HEB; JAS; PHIL; PHILEM; ROM; TIT	likely	PROB
		likewise	DO
		Lima	L
		limited	LTD
letter of credit	LC	limited company	BV; GMBH; PLC; SA
letters	COR; PET; THESS; TIM	limited liability	ANME
		limner	RA
letting agents	ARLA	Lincoln	ABE

Lincolnshire	LINCS	local education authority	LEA
line	L; *see also* railway	local management of schools	LMS
line feed	LF	locality	EC; NE; NW; SE; SW
line of communication	LOFC		
lineal	LIN	loch	L
linear	LIN	lodger	PG
liner	RMS	logarithm	LN; LOG
lines	LL; *see also* railway	logarithm odds	LOD
		logisticians	RLC
lines per minute	LPM	London	LOND
linguistics	LING	London: part of London	E; EC; N; NW; SE; SW; W; WC
Linnaean	LINN		
Linnaean Society	LS	London: of London	LONDIN
Linnaeus	LINN	long	L
liquid	AQ; LIQ	Long Island	LI
liquid crystal display	LCD	long metre	LM
liquor	LIQ	long wave	LW
lira	L; LR	longitude	LON; LONG
lire	L	long-playing	LP
literal	LIT	loop	O
literally	LIT	lord	D; DOM; LD
literary	LIT	Lord Birkenhead	FE
literary paper	TLS	Lord Chief Justice	LCJ
Literate in Arts	LA	Lord Justice	LJ
literature	LIT	Lord Lieutenant	LL
literature society	RSL	Lord Mayor	LM
lithium	LI	Lord Privy Seal	LPS
Lithuania	LITH; LT	Lord Provost	LP
Lithuanian	LITH	lordship	LDP
litre(s)	L	Los Angeles	LA
little time	MO; S; SEC	loss of independent existence	LIE
live	L		
lived; lived so many years	AV	lot	C; D; K; L; M
		lots	C; D; K; L; M
Liverpool	LPOOL	lottery regulator	NLC
load(s)	C; D; K; L; M	loud	F
loan	SUB	Lough	L
local	PH; PUB		
local area network	LAN		

full form ⇨ abbreviation

Louis	LEW	low-level waste	LLW
Louisa; Louise	LOU	low-water mark	LWM
Louisiana	LA	loyalists	DUP; UU
love	O	lubricant	PET
low	B	Ludovic; Ludovick	LEW
Low Dutch	LD	lumen	LM; LU
low frequency	LF	luminance	L
Low German	LG	Lunar Excursion Module	LEM
Low Latin	LL	lunar module	LM
low pressure	LP	lunch time	l
low tension	LT	luncheon voucher	LV
lowdown	GEN; INF	lunchtime	PM
lower case	LC	lutetium	LU
lower house	HC	lux	LX
lowest common denominator	LCD	Luxembourg	L
lowest common multiple	LCM		

mac	M; MC	Maltese cross	GC
Maccabees	MACC	man	B; G; GBM; IOM; K; KT; M; MR; N; P; Q; R; *see also* Appendix: First Names
Macedonia	MK		
machine readable cataloguing	MARC		
machine-finished	MF	management buy-in	MBI
machine-gun	MG	management buy-out	MBO
machinery	MACH	manager	ACMA; CCMI; MD; MGR
Madagascar	RM		
madam	M	managing	IC
madame	MDM; MME	managing director	MANDIR; MD
made: he/she made	FEC	manganese	MN
made: they made	FF	Manitoba	MB
mademoiselle	MDLLE; MLLE	man-machine interaction; man-machine interface	MMI
magazine	MAG; TES; TLS		
magistrate	JP	manpower economics office	OME
magnesium	MAG; MG		
magnetic	MAG	manufactured	MFD
magnetic field strength	H	manufacturers	MFRS
magnetic flux density	B	manuscript	MS
magnetism	MAG	manuscripts	MSS
magneto-optical	MO	Manx	IOM
magnitude	MAG	Manx parliament	HK
maiden; maiden over	M	many	C; CD; D; K; L; M
mail	E	map-makers	OS
main force	RN	March	MAR
main road	A1; A1M; M1	Margaret	MAG; MEG; PEG
Maine	ME	margin; marginal	MARG
maître	ME	Maria; Marie	MAY
major	MAJ	marine(s)	RM
make up	ADLIB	marine nature reserve	MNR
Malachi	MAL	mariner(s)	*see* sailor *and* sailors
Malawi	MW		
Malaysia	MAL	mark	DM; M; MB; MK; NB
male	M		
male chauvinist pig	MCP	mark of the Beast	MB
Mali	RMM	mark well	NB
Malta	M	market	CACM; CARICOM; EC; EEC; MKT

markka	MK	mean time	MT
married	M	means of identification	DNA
marsupial	ROO	measles, mumps and rubella	MMR
marvellous	FAB		
Mary	MAY	measure	F; FT; LB; M; Y; YD; *see also* unit
Maryland	MD		
masculine	M; MAS; MASC	measure of intelligence	IQ
mass	M	meat and bone meal	MBM
Massachusetts	MA; MASS	mechanical	MECH
master	M; MA; ME; *see also* Appendix: Degrees	mechanical engineer	ME
		mechanical transport	MT
		mechanics	MECH
Master of Arts	AM; MA	medal	DSO; GC; MC; MM; VC; *see also* Appendix: Decorations
Master of Ceremonies	MC		
Master of Laws	LLM		
Master of Surgery	CHM; CM; MCH; MS		
		mediators	ACAS
Master of the Rolls	MR	medic	*see* doctor
Mathilda; Matilda	MAT	medical	MED
matinée	MAT	medical insurers	BUPA
matrix	MAT	medical man	*see* doctor
Matthew; Matthias	MAT	medical officer	DMO; MO; MOH; PMO; SMO
Maureen	MO		
Mauritania	RIM	medical solvent	DMSO
Mauritian rupee	MR	medical specialism	ECG; ENT; MRI; OT; REHAB
Mauritius	MS		
Maximilian	MAX	medicine	MED
maximum	MAX	medicine society	RSM
maxwell	MX	medico	*see* doctor
mayday	SOS	medieval	MED
Mayfair	W1	Mediterranean	MED
mbar(s)	MB	medium	FT; M; MED; TV
McDonalds	M	medium frequency	MF
me	I	medium wave	MW
meal ready to eat	MRE	meeting	AGM; EGM
meal ticket	LV	meeting place	RV
meals ready to eat	MRE	meg(s)	MB; MBYTE
mean lethal dose	MLD	megabyte(s)	MB; MBYTE
mean sea-level	MSL	megacycles per second	MCS

full form ⇨ abbreviation

mega-electronvolt(s)	MEV	metal	*see* Appendix: Chemical Elements
megahertz	MHZ		
megajoule(s)	MJ	metal oxide semiconductor	MOS
megavolt(s)	MV		
megawatt	MW	metalloid	AS; B; GE; PO; SB; SE; SI; TE
meitnerium	MT		
melting-point	MP	metallurgical; metallurgy	METAL; METALL
member	AM; M; MBE; MEM; MEP; MP; MSP		
		metaphor; metaphorical	MET; METAPH
Member of Congress	MC	metaphysical; metaphysics	MET; METAPH
Member of Council	MC		
Member of Parliament	MEP; MP; MSP; TD	meteorological	MET
		meteorologists	RMS
member of union	*see* Appendix: US States	meteorology	MET; METEOR
		method of working	MO
memento	MEM	Methodist Episcopal	ME
memorandum	MEM	metical	MT; MZM
memorandum of understanding	MOU	metre(s)	M
		metre-kilogram-second	MKS
memorial	MEM	metric carat	CM
memory	DRAM; EDO; EDORAM; EEPROM; EMS; EPROM; EROM; PROM; RAM; ROM; SRAM; VRAM	Metro	M
		metropolitan	MET
		Metropolitan Police	MET; MP
		Mexican; Mexico	MEX
		mezzo-forte	MF
memory address register	MAR	mezzo-piano	MP
		mica	MIC
men	OR	Micah	MIC
mendelevium	MD; MV	Michaelmas	MICH
mentally deficient	MD	Michigan	MI; MICH
Merchant Navy	MN	micron	MU
merchant vessel	MV	microscope	SEM; TEM
mercury	HG	Mid Glamorgan	MGLAM
meridiem	M	midday	M; N
Merseyside	NW	middle	MED
message	MEM	middle combination room; middle common room	MCR
Messerschmitt	ME		
messieurs	MM		

Middle East	ME	Minimum Use of Force Tactical Intervention	MUFTI
Middle English	ME		
Middle French	MF	mining company	RTZ
Middlesex	MIDDX; MX	mining engineer	ME
midheaven	MC	minister	MIN; *see also* clergyman
midnight	OAM		
midshipman	MID	ministry	MAFF; METI; MGB; MIN; MOD; MOH
midwife	SCM		
Mike	M		
mile(s)	M; MI; ML	Minnesota	MINN; MN
miles per gallon	MPG	minor friars	OFM
miles per hour	MPH	Minority Rights Group	MRG
militants	ETA	minute(s)	M; MIN
military	MIL; MILIT	miscellaneous	MISC
Military Cross	MC	miserable; misery	MIZ
military decoration	*see* Appendix: Decorations	miss	MDLLE; MLLE
		missile	AAM; ABM; AGM; ALCM; AMRAAM; ASBM; ASM; ATM; GLCM; ICBM; IRBM; MRBM; SAM; SLBM; SSM; TASM; V1
military intelligence	MI		
military medal	MC; MM		
military police	MP		
military postal service	BFPO		
milk	TT; UHT		
millibar(s)	MB		
milligram(s); milligramme(s)	MG	missile defence alarm system	MIDAS
		missile experimental	MX
millilitre(s)	ML	missing	AWOL; MIA
millimetre(s)	MM	mission	OP
millimole(s)	MMOL	Mississippi	MISS; MS
million(s)	M	Missouri	MO
millions of instructions per second	MIPS	Mister	MR
		Mistress	MRS
millisecond(s)	MS	mo	S; SEC
millisievert(s)	MSV	mobile identification number	MIN
miners	IMO; NUM; UDM		
		model	T
miniature circuit breaker	MCB	moderate	MOD; OK
minimum	MIN	moderate speed	MOD

full form	abbreviation	full form	abbreviation
moderately loud	MF	Morris Garages	MG
moderately quiet	MP	mortgage interest relief	MIR; MIRAS
moderately soft	MP	most excellent	A1; ME
moderato	MOD	Most Holy Lord	SSD
modern	AD; MOD	most significant bit	MSB
modern times	AD	most valuable player	MVP
modus operandi	MO	mother	MA; MAM; MOM; MUM
molar latent heat	L	motivation research; motivational research	MR
Moldova	MD		
mole	MOL	motor race	TT
molecular weight	MOLWT	motor vessel	MV
molybdenum	MO	motor yacht	MY
moment	MO	motoring organization; motorists	AA; AAA; RAC
Monaco	MC		
monarch	CR; ER; GR; HM; K; Q; R	motorway	AB; M; M1
Monday	M; MON	motorway service area	MSA
money	L; LSD; M; P	mount	GG; MT
money order	MO	mountain	MT
Mongolia	MGL	Mountain Time	MT
monk(s)	OFM; OSA; OSB; OSF	mounted police	MP
		mounties	MP
Monmouthshire	MON	moving target detector	MTD
Monseigneur	MGR	Mozambique	MOC
monsieur	M	Mozart's works	K
Monsignor; Monsignore	MGR; MONSIG; MSGR	multi-frequency	MF
		multilateral force	MLF
Montana	MONT; MT	multinational; multinational chemical company	BASF; ICI
Montgomeryshire	MONT		
month	APR; AUG; AV; DEC; FEB; JAN; JUL; JUN; JY; M; MAR; MO; MTH; NOV; OCT; SEP; SEPT	multiplex analogue components	MAC
		municipal police	MP
		muscle	AB; LAT; PEC
months	M; MOS	muses	IX
Moral Rearmament	MRA	museum	BM; MOMA; MOMI; MUS; VA; VANDA
more or less	C; CA		
morning	AM		
Morocco	MA; MOR	music	AOR; MOR; MUS

music television	MTV	mutual assured destruction	MAD
musical	MUS	muzzle velocity	MV
musical instrument	SAX; UKE	my	M
musical piece	OP	Myanmar	MYA; UOM
musician	BMUS; DMUS; LLCM; LRAM; MMUS; MUSB; MUSD	mystery	UFO
musicians	ABRSM; RAM; RCM; RIAM; RSM		

nag	GG	National Olympic Committee	NOC
Nahum	NAH	national statistics office	ONS
naira	N	National Theatre	NT
name	N	National Trust	NT
name unknown	ANON; NU	nationalist	N; NAT
namely	SC; SCIL; SCIZ; VIZ	nationalists	BJP; BNP; INLA; SNP
Namibia	NAM	native	NAT
nanometre(s)	NM	natural	NAT
nanosecond(s)	NS	natural killer	NK
napoleon	NAP	natural language processing	NLP
Nathan; Nathaniel	NAT	natural logarithm	LN
national	N; NAT	natural order	NO
National Academy of Sciences	NAS	naturalists	LS
National Air Traffic Services	NATS	Nature Conservancy Council	NCC
National Audit Office	NAO	naught	O
National Car Parks	NCP	Nauru	NAU
National Childbirth Trust	NCT	nautical	NAUT
National Curriculum	NC	nautical measure	KN; NM
national emergency action committee	COBRA	nautical mile	NM
National Energy Foundation	NEF	naval	NAV
		naval air service	RNAS
National Engineering Laboratory	NEL	naval air station	RNAS
		naval reserve	RNR
National Film Theatre	NFT	navigable; navigation	NAV
		navigator	NAV
National Guard	NG	navy	N; RAN; RCN; RN; USN; WRANS
National Health Insurance	NHI		
National Institute for Clinical Excellence	NICE	Nazi élite corps	SS
		Nazi terrorist militia	SA
National Institutes of Health	NIH	near	NR
		Nebraska	NB; NE; NEB; NEBR
national insurance	NI		
national insurance contributions	NIC	negative; negatively	NEG
		negotiable	NEG

full form ⇨ abbreviation

full form	abbreviation	full form	abbreviation
Nehemiah	NEH	new series	NS
neighbour	BOR	New South Wales	NSW
neodymium	ND	New Style	NS
neon	NE	New Testament	NT
Nepal	NEP	new version	NV
neptunium	NP	New York	NY
net asset value	NAV	New York City	NYC
Net Book Agreement	NBA	New York Stock Exchange	NYSE
net national product	NNP	New Zealand	NZ
net present value	NPV	newcomer	DEB
net realizable value	NRV	Newfoundland	NF
net weight	NTWT	newly industrialized country	NIC
The Netherlands	NETH; NL	news agency	AP; TASS
Netherlands Antilles	NA	newsman	ED; SUB
network	ABC; BBC; CBS; DIANE; ITV; LAN; MAN; NBC; PSTN; WAN; WWW	newspaper	FT
		newspaperman	ED; SUB
		newton(s)	N
network computer	NC	next month	PROX
neurolinguistic programming	NLP	ngultrum	N; NU
		Nicaragua	NIC
neuter; neutral	N; NEUT	nickel	NI
neutron	N	nicotine patch	NAD
Nevada	NEV; NV	nielsbohrium	NS
never-never	HP	Niger	RN
new	N	Nigeria	NGR
new books	NT	nil	O
New Brunswick	NB	nine	IX
new driver	L	nineteen	XIX
New England	NE	ninety	N; XC
New General Catalogue	NGC	ninety thousand	N
New Hampshire	NH	ninety-nine	IC
New Jersey	NJ	niobium	NB
New Mexico	NM; NMEX	nitrogen	N
New Orleans	NO	nitrogen oxide	NOX
new paragraph	NP	no	O
New Providence	NP	no charge	NC

full form ⇨ abbreviation

no date	ND
no funds	NF
no good	NG; US
no place	NP
no sex	N
no trumps	NT
no value declared	NVD
no-ball	NB
nobelium	NO
noble; nobleman	BT; MARQ
Noise Abatement Society	NAS
Noise and Number Index	NNI
noisy	F
nom de plume	PSEUD
nominal	NOM
nominative	N; NOM
non sequitur	NONSEQ
non-accidental injury	NAI
non-commissioned officer	CPL; LCPL; NCO; RSM; SERG; SERGT; SERJ; SERJT; SGT; SM; WO
non-drinker(s)	AA; TT
non-governmental organization	NGO
nonsense	BS
non-smoker	NS
non-specific urethritis	NSU
noon	M; N
normal	NORM
normal temperature and pressure	NTP
Norman	NOR; NORM
Norman French	NF
Norse	N
north	N; NOR; NTH
North America	NA

North Atlantic Treaty Organization	NATO
North Britain; North British	NB
North Carolina	NC
North Dakota	ND; NDAK
North Island	NI
North Warning System	NWS
Northamptonshire	NORTHANTS
north-east	NE
north-eastern	NE
northern	N
Northern French	NF
Northern Ireland	NI
Northern Territory	NT
north-north-east	NNE
north-north-west	NNW
Northumberland	NORTHUMB
north-west	NW
Northwest Territories	NT; NW
north-western	NW
Norway	N; NO; NOR
Norwegian	NOR
not	NT
not a lot	I; II; III; IV; IX; V; VI; VII; VIII
not applicable	NA
not available	NA
not dated	ND
not far	NL
not for sale	NFS
not out	NO
not specified	NS
not sufficient funds	NSF
nota bene	NB
Notary Public	NP

note	A; B; C; D; DO; DOH; E; F; FA; FAH; G; H; LA; LAH; ME; MEM; MI; N; NB; RAY; RE; SI; SO; SOH; SOL; TE; TI; UT	nuclear, biological and chemical	NBC
		nuclear magnetic resonance	NMR
		nuclear ship	NS
		nucleolar-organizing region	NOR
note well	NB	number	N; NO; NUM; PIN; *see also* Appendix: Roman Numerals
Notes and Queries	NANDQ		
nothing; nothing at all	FA; O; SFA; Z		
nothing doing	NIX		
notice	AD	numbers	NOS; NUM; NUMB
Nottinghamshire	NOTTS		
nought	O	numeral	NUM
noun	N	numerical control	NC
noun phrase	NP	nurse	CNN; EN; ENG; RGN; RMN; RN; SEN; SNO; SRN
Nova Scotia	NS		
November	N; NOV		
novice	L	nurses	RCN; VAD
now; nowadays	AD	Nursing and Midwifery Council	NMC
nuclear	N; NUC	nutritionists	SACN

Obadiah	OBAD	of the same	EJUSD
obedient	OBDT	of Winchester	WINTON
object	OBJ	of Worcester	WIGORN
object linking and embedding	OLE	of York	EBOR
		offers over	OO
objective	OBJ	office	*see* toilet
objector	CO	Office of Communications	OFCOM
object-oriented programming	OOP	officer	CO; FO; LT; MO; OC; OFF; PO; WO; *see also* Appendix: Serviceman, Servicewoman
obligation	IOU		
oblique	OBL		
oblong	OBL		
obscure	OBS		
observation	OBS	Officer Cadet Training Unit	OCTU
observation point; observation post	OP		
		Officer Commanding	OC
observe	NB	Officer in Charge	OC
observers	ROC	Officer of (the Order of) Australia	AO
obsessive-compulsive disorder	OCD		
		Officer of the Day	OD
obsolete	OBS	Officers' Training Corps	OTC
obstetric treatment	DANDC		
occupational therapist	OT; ROT	official	OFF
occupational therapy	OT	officinal	OFF
octavo	OCT	Offshore Industry Liaison Committee	OILC
October	OCT		
Oddfellow	OF	oh, I see	OIC
odds	SP	Ohio	O; OH
odour	BO	oil company	BP; ESSO
oersted	OE	okay	OK
of	O	Oklahoma	OK; OKLA
of Cambridge	CANTAB	old	O
of Durham	DUNELM	old books	OT
of Ely	ELIEN	old boy	OB
of Exeter	EXON	Old English	OE
of her/his age	AE; AET	old flame	EX
of London	LONDIN	Old French	OF
of Oxford	OXON	Old High German	OHG
of St Albans	ALBAN	old man	*see* dad

O

full form ⇨ abbreviation

Old Measurement	OM
Old Norse	ON
old pence; old penny	D; OP
old soldier	VET
Old Style	OS
Old Testament	OT
old-age pensioner	OAP
olympic committee	IOC; NOC
omega	O
omicron	O
on	O; RE
on account of	OA
on active service	OAS
On Her/His Majesty's Service	OHMS
on the wagon	TT
on view to all	U
one	A; I; J
one coming out	DEB
one member one vote	OMOV
one o'clock	NNE
one-day international	ODI
one-time	EX
only child	OC
on-target earnings	OTE
Ontario	ON
oomph	SA
open	OPE
Open University	OU
open-ended investment company	OEIC
opera; opera house	ENO; ROH; MET
operating system	BIOS; CPM; DOS; MSDOS®; OS
operation	OP
operational research	OR
operations	OPS
operations officer	OPS
operations research	OR

operations room	OPS
operator	OP
opponent	E; N; S; W
opponents	EN; ES; NE; NW; SE; SW; WN; WS
oppose; opposed	OPP
opposed to; opposing	V; VS
opposite	OP; OPP
opposite prompt	OP
optative	OPT
optic; optical	OPT
optical character reader; optical character reading; optical character recognition	OCR
optical mark recognition	OMR
optimum	OPT
optional	OPT
opus	OP
or	AU
or near offer; or nearest offer	ONO
oral rehydration therapy	ORT
orchestra	CBSO; ECO; LPO; LSO; NYO; NYOS; ORCH; RPO; RSNO
orchestrated by	ORCH
ordained	ORD
order	DSO; OBE; OM; OP; ORD; OSA; OSB; PO; *see also* Appendix: Decorations
Order of Canada	OC
Order of Merit	OM
Order of Preachers	OP
Order of the Bath	OB

Order of the British Empire	OBE	otorhinolaryngology	ENT
ordinary	O; ORD	ought	O
ordinary seaman	OS	ounce	OZ
ordnance	ORD	ounces	OZ; OZS
ordnance data; ordnance datum	OD	our era; our time	AD
		out of bounds	OB
Ordnance Survey	OS	out of date	OBS
Oregon	OR; OREG	out of print	OP
organists	RCO	out of this world	ET
organization	*see* company	outside broadcast	OB
Organization of African Unity	AU; OAU	outsize	OS; XL
		oval	O
Organization of American States	OAS	oven	AGA
		over	OER
Organization of French Settlers	OAS	over 18	X
		over the counter	OTC
organophosphate	OP	over the top	OTT
orient; oriental	E	overcharge	OC
origin	ORIG	overdose	OD
original	ORIG	overdraft	OD
original cover	OC	overdrawn	OD
original equipment manufacturer	OEM	overhead projector	OHP
		Overseas Development Administration	ODA
originally	ORIG		
Oscar	O	Oxford: of Oxford	OXON
osmium	OS	Oxford University	OU
other people's	OPS	Oxfordshire	OXON
other ranks	OR	oxygen	O
otherwise	AKA	Oz	*see* Australia

Pacific Standard Time	PST	Parish Council	PC
Pacific Time	PT	parish priest	PP
pacifist	CO	park	PK
pack	PK	parking	P
packet switching system	PSS	parliament	HC; HK; HL; HP; HR; PARL
page	F; P; RO; VO	parliamentarian	AM; MEP; MP; MSP; TD
page description language	PDL	parliamentary	PARL
pages	FF; PP	Parliamentary Private Secretary	PPS
paid	PD	Parliamentary Secretary	PPS
painted: he/she painted	PINX	parochial church council	PCC
painter	ARA; RA	parson	MIN; P; PP; PR; RD; RECT; REV; REVD
pair	OO; PR		
Pakistan	PAK; PK		
Pakistani	PAK	part	PT
Palestinian National Authority	PNA	participle	P
palladium	PD	partner	E; N; S; SOP; W
Pamela	PAM	partners	EW; NS; SN; WE
Pan-Africanist Congress	PAC	Partnership for Peace	PFP
Panama	PA	parts per million	PPM
papa	P	party	ALP; BJP; BNP; C; CLP; CON; CP; D; DEM; DLP; DUP; EPP; GOP; IFP; KANU; L; LAB; LIB; LIBDEM; LP; NF; PASOK; PGB; PLP; RPR; SDLP; SDP; SF; SLD; SNP; SPD; SWAPO; SWP; UU; WRP
paper	FT		
paperback	PB		
Papua New Guinea	PNG		
paragon	*see* saint		
paragraph	PAR; PARA		
Paraguay	PY		
parallel	PAR		
paramilitary	SAS		
paratrooper	PARA	pascal	P; PA
parental guidance	PG	pass	COP
Parents Against Injustice	PAIN	passed	OK
		passed staff college	PSC
Parent-Teacher Association	PTA	Passenger Transport Authority	PTA
parish	PAR		

full form ⇨ abbreviation

P

Passenger Transport Executive	PTE	Pennsylvania	PA; PENN
		penny	D; P
passenger-carrying vehicle	PCV	pennyweight	PWT
		pension	SIPP
passive	PASS	pension scheme	SERPS
past	PA; PT	pensioner	OAP
past grand master	PGM	peptide nucleic acid	PNA
past master	PM	per	EA; PR
past participle	PAP; PP	per annum	PA; PERAN
past president	PP	per calendar month	PCM
past tense	PAT; PT	per cent	PC; PCT
pastor	P	per pro	PP
patent	PAT	per week	PW
patent agents	CIPA	perceived noise decibel	PNDB
patented	PAT	perfect	A1; PERF
pathological; pathology	PATH; PATHOL	performance-related pay	PRP
Patricia	PAT	Performing Rights Society	PRS
Patrick	PAT		
Patriotic Front	PF	perhaps	PERH
pawn	P	period	PER
pay as you earn	PAYE	periodical	MAG; TES; TLS
pay on delivery	POD	peripheral component interconnect	PCI
paying guest	PG		
paymaster	PMR	permanent health insurance	PHI
Paymaster General	PMG		
payment system	BACS; CHAPS	permanent interest-bearing share	PIBS
peacekeepers	KFOR; UN		
peacemaker(s)	ACAS	permanent vegetative state	PVS
peak	MT; PK		
peck	PK	Persian	PERS
pedal	P	persistent organic pollutant	POP
pedestrian	PED		
peeler	*see* policeman	persistent vegetative state	PVS
pen	J		
pen-name	PSEUD	person	BOD; PER; PERS
pence	D, P	person with AIDS	PWA
Penelope	PEN	personal	PERS
peninsula	PEN	personal appearance	PA
penitentiary	PEN	personal assistant	PA

personal computer	PC	philology	PHIL
personal digital assistant	PDA	philosopher	BPHIL; DPH; DPHIL; MPHIL; PHD
personal equity plan	PEP	philosophical; philosophy	PHIL
personal flotation device	PFD	philosophy, politics and economics	PPE
personal identification number	PIN	phone, *etc*	*see* telephone, *etc*
personal information manager	PIM	phonetics	PHON; PHONET
Personal Investment Authority	PIA	phonography	PHONOG
		phosphorus	P
personal trainer; personal training	PT	photo; photograph	PIC
		photoelectric cell	PEC
personnel	HR	photographer	FRPS
Peru	PE	photographers	RPS
peseta	P; PES; PTA	photographic; photography	PHOT
peso	P	photomechanical transfer	PMT
Peter	PET		
petty officer	CPO; PO	phrase	PHR
pfennig	PF	physical education	PE
pharmaceutical	PHAR; PHARM	physical jerks	*see* jerks
Pharmaceutical Society	PS	physical therapy	PT
		physical training	PT
pharmacist	BPHARM; MPHARM; MPS; MRPHARMS	physically handicapped and able bodied	PHAB
pharmacists	PS	physician	FRCP; PHYS; *see also* doctor
Pharmacopoeia Britannica	PB		
		physics	PHYS
phase alternation line	PAL	physics laboratory	NPL
Philadelphia	PHIL	physiology	PHYS
Philemon	PHILEM	physiotherapists	CSP
Philip; Phillip	PHIL; PIP	pianissimo	PP
Philippians	PHIL	pianississimo	PPP
Philippines	RP	piano	P
Phillip	*see* Philip	pianoforte	PF
philological	PHIL	pick-up	PU
Philological Society	PS	pick-your-own	PYO
philologist	MPS		

P

picture	PIC	point of sale terminal	POST
picture postcard	PPC	point of view	POV
pictures	PICS; PIX	Poland	PL
piece	B; K; KT; N; P; PCE; Q; R	pole	N; PO; S
		poles	NS; SN
pilot officer	PO	police	AP; CIB; CID; KGB; KP; LAPD; MET; MGB; MP; NYPD; OGPU; PD; PSNI; RCMP; RIC; RMP; RUC; SS; SWAT
pilots	ALPA; BALPA		
pink paper	FT		
pint(s)	PT		
pious	PI		
place	PL		
plain old telephone system	POTS	Police and Criminal Evidence Act	PACE
plan position indicator	PPI	police chiefs	ACPO; ACPOS
Planck's constant	H	police constable	PC
plane	*see* aircraft	police department	PD
planned activities time	PAT	policeman; police officer	DC; DI; DS; PC; PS; SC; TEC
plastic	PET; PTFE; PVC		
plastic providers	AMEX	police sergeant	PS
plate	EPNS; L; T	policewoman	PW; WPC; *see also* policeman
platinum	PT		
play	RUR	political and economic planning	PEP
player	E; N; S; W		
players	11; RSC; XI; XV; *see also* orchestra	political correctness	PC
		political economy	POLECON
pleasant Sunday afternoon	PSA	politically correct	PC
		politically correct retailing	PCR
please turn over	PTO		
plug	AD; ADVT	politician	AM; CON; LAB; LIB; MEP; MP; MSP; TD
pluperfect	PLUP		
plural	PL; PLU; PLUR		
plutonium	PU	pollsters	MORI; NOP
Plymouth	PL	pollutant	PCB
Plymouth Brethren	PB	polonium	PO
poet	AE; PL	polymer	PHB
Poet Laureate	PL	polymerase chain reaction	PCR
point	E; N; PT; S; W	pony	TAT
point of presence	POP	pop(s)	*see* dad
point of sale	POS	Pope	SSD

full form ⇨ abbreviation

poppet	POP	potentiometer	POT
popular	POP	pound	L; LB; SOV
popularly	POP	pound force	LBF
population	POP	pound(s) sterling	L
port	L; PT; RIO	pounds	L; LB
Port of London Authority	PLA	pounds, shillings and pence	LSD
portable document format	PDF	powder	PULV
		power	P
portable network graphic	PNG	power-on-self-test	POST
portrait gallery	NPG	praise be to God always	LDS
portrait painters	RP	praseodymium	PR
Portugal	P; PG	prebend; prebendary	PREB
Portuguese	PG	pre-delivery inspection	PDI
poser	Q; QU	preface	PREF
posh	U	preference	PREF
position	POS	preferred	PREF
positive	P; POS	premenstrual tension	PMT
post and packing	PANDP	premier	PM
post meridiem	PM	premium	AP; PM
post mortem	PM	premium bond picker	ERNIE
post office	GPO; PO	preparation	PREP
post office preferred	POP	preposition	PREP
postage and packing	PANDP; PP	Presbyterian	UP
postal order	PO	Pre-School Learning Alliance	PLA
postal service	RM	Pre-School Playgroups Association	PPA
postal telegraph	PT	present	PR; PRES
postcard	PC	present day	AD
poster	AD; ADVT	present time	AD; DEC
postmaster	PM	present month	DEC; INST
Postmaster General	PMG	present pupil	PP
postnatal depression	PND	Preservation of the Rights of Prisoners	PROP
postscript	PS		
post-town	PT	preservationists	ACE; BTCV; CPRE; FOE; NT; RSNC; RSPB; SPAB
potassium	K		
potential energy	PE		
potentially exempt transfer	PET		

president	ABE; FDR; IKE; P; PRES	Private Finance Initiative	PFI
President of the Royal Society	PRS	private first class	PFC
		private investigator	PI
press	AAP; AP; CUP; OUP; PA	Private Patients' Plan	PPP
		private secretary	PS
press agency	AFP; AP; TASS	private sector liquidity	PSL
Press Association	PA	privileged	U
Press Complaints Commission	PCC	privy councillor	PC
		prize ring	PR
press employee	ED; SUB	probable	PROB
press release	PR	probation officers	NAPO
pressman	ED; SUB	probationary driver	P
pressure	P	procurator fiscal	PF
pressurized water reactor	PWR	professional	PRO
		professor	PROF; RP; STP
price	PR	professor of theology	STP
price-earnings ratio	PE	profit before interest and tax	PBIT
priest	HP; P; PP; PR; *see also* clergyman	profit-related pay	PRP
prime minister	PM	programme evaluation and review technique	PERT
prince	P; PR		
Prince Edward Island	PE	programming language	APL; COL; HTML; IAL; JCL; PDL; PL; QL; RPG; SGML; SQL; VRML; WML; XML
princess	DI		
principal	1ST; PRIN		
principal clerk of session	PCS		
principal medical officer	PMO	progress of life	CV
		promethium	PM
print	LITH; LITHO	promise	IOU
printing	LITH; LITHO; LITHOG	promissory note	IOU; PN
		promotion	*see* advert
prison	HMP; PEN	prompt side	PS
Prison Officers' Association	POA	proper; properly	PROP
		property	PROP
prisoner	CON; POW	Property Services Agency	PSA
prisoner of Mother England	POM		
private	GI; PTE	proportional representation	PR
private automatic exchange	PAX		

proposition	PROP	public company	PLC
proprietary	PTY	public house	PH
proprietor	PROP	public lending right	PLR
prosecutor	DA	public library	PL
prosecutors	CPS	public limited company	PLC
prospective parliamentary candidate	PPC	public private partnership	PPP
prostitute	PRO	Public Record Office	PRO
protactinium	PA	public relations	PR
protectionists	DPA; RSPB; SPAB; SPUC	public relations officer	PRO
		public service vehicle	PSV
Protective Squad	SS	Public Services Authority	PSA
protein	AAT; AFP; HDL; LDL; SCP	public telecommunications operator	PTO
Protestant	PROT	public works department	PWD
Protestant Episcopal	PE		
Provençal	PR	public works office	OPW
Provence	PROV	publicity	AD; ADVT
proverbs	PROV	publicity agent	PA
province	*see* Canadian province	publishers	APA; CUP; HMSO; IPA; IPC; NPA; OUP; UPI
Province of Quebec	PQ		
provincial	PROV	Publishers Association	PA
provisional	IRA	Puerto Rico	PR
provisional driver	P	puff	AD; ADVT
provost	PROV	pula	P
provost marshal	PM	pulled up	PU
proxy	PP	pulse code modulation	PCM
psalm; psalms	PS	pulsed electro magnetic energy	PEME
psi	PS		
psychiatric social worker	PSW	punch	KO
		pupil	L
psychokinesis	PK	pupil teacher	PT
psychologists	BPS	purchase tax	PT
pub	PH	purl	P
public access mobile radio	PAMR	purple heart	PH
		pyjamas	PJS
public address; public address system	PA		

Q

Qatar	Q	quasar	QSO
qualified teacher status	QTS	quasi-stellar object	QSO
quality	Q	Quebec	PQ; Q; QUE
quality assurance	QA	queen	ER; FD; HM; Q; QU; R
quality assurance data system	QADS	Queen and Empress	RI
quality circle	QC	Queen Elizabeth	ER
quality control	QC	Queen Elizabeth Hall	QEH
quality-adjusted life year	QALY	Queen Victoria	VR
quantity	AMT; QT; QTY; VOL	Queen's Bench	QB
		Queen's College	QC
quantum chromodynamics	QCD	Queen's Counsel	QC
		queen's son	P
quantum electrodynamics	QED	Queensland	Q; QLD
		query	Q; QY
quart	Q; QT; QU; QUAR	query language	QL
		question	Q; QU
quarter	E; N; Q; QR; QU; QUAR; S; W	quetzal	Q
		quid	L; SOV
quarter day	LD	quiet	P; QT
quarter-inch cartridge	QIC	quintal	Q; QL
quarterly	QU; QUAR	quintet	V
quartermaster	QM	quotation	QUOT
quarto	Q; QTO		

rabbinical	RABB	rather loud; rather loudly	MF
race	GP; TT	rather quiet; rather soft	MP
Rachael; Rachel	RAE; RAY	Raymond	RAE; RAY
radian	RAD	reactor	AGR
radiator	RAD	reader	ABC
radiators, boilers, *etc*	CH	reading	R
radical	RAD	ready	L; LSD; P
radio	CB	ream	RM
radio data system	RDS	rear admiral	RA
radio direction finder; radio direction finding	RDF	Réaumur's thermometric scale	R; REAU
radio frequency	RF	Rebecca	BEX
radio telegraphy	RT	receipt	REC; RECPT; REPT
radio telephony	RT	received	RECD
radioimmunoassay	RIA	Received Pronunciation	RP
radiologists	RCR	Rechabite	TT
radium	RA	recipe	R; REC
radius	R; RAD	recognized investment exchanges	RIE
radon	RN	recognized professional body	RPB
Rail Passengers' Council	RPC	recommended daily allowance	RDA
rail regulator's office	ORR	recommended dietary allowance	RDA
railroad	EL; L	recommended retail price	RRP
railway	BR; CPR; EL; EWS; GNER; GWR; L; LMS; LNE; LNER; RLY; RWY; RY; SNCF; SR	record	CAD; CD; DVD; EP; LP; REC
railwaymen	ASLEF; NUR	record company	BMG; EMI; HMV
rand	R	record distributor	HMV
rapid eye movement	REM	record player	DJ
rate	AER; APR; BPM; BPS; BR; CAR; CNAR; CPM; CPS; CS; FPS; KMH; KPG; KPH; LIBOR; LPM; MCS; MIPS; MPG; MPH; RPM; RPS; UBR; WPM	record producer	BMG; EMI
		record shop	HMV
		recorder	CCR; VCR; VTR
		recording	*see* record
		recreation	REC

full form	abbreviation	full form	abbreviation
recreation ground	REC	Register of Friendly Societies	RFS
recreational vehicle	RV	registered	REGD
recto	RO	registered nurse	RN
rector	R; RECT	registration number	REG
rectory	RECT	Regius Professor	RP
Red Cross	RC	regulator	FSA; NLC
redcap	MP	rehabilitate; rehabilitation	REHAB
reduced instruction set computer	RISC	rehabilitation centre	REHAB
redundancy order	LIFO; LILO	related; relating	REL
redundant array of independent disks; redundant array of inexpensive disks	RAID	relation; relative	BRO; COZ; DA; DAD; MA; MAM; MOM; MUM; NAN; PA; POP; REL; SIB; SIS
refer to drawer	RD		
referee	REF; UMP	relative atomic mass	RAM
reference	REF	relative density	RELD
reference library	RL	Relative Strength Index	RSI
reflection; reflective	REFL		
reflex	REFL	religion	CE; RC
reflexive	REFL	religious	PI; see also monk(s)
Reformed Church	REFCH		
reformed drinkers	AA	religious book(s)	NT; OT
Reformed Episcopal	RE	religious education	RE
Reformed Presbyterian	RP	religious instruction; religious teaching	RI
refugee	DP		
regarding	RE	remember	MEM; NB
regiment	RA; RE; REGT; REME; RGT	remote guidance vehicle	RGV
regimental court martial	RCM	remote job entry	RJE
		remote job entry terminal	RJET
Regina	R		
Reginald	REG; REX	remotely-operated vehicle	ROV
regional electricity company	REC	remotely-piloted vehicle	RPV
regional health authority	RHA		
		rendezvous	RV
regionally important geological site	RIGS	repeat	REP; RPT
		repertory	REP
		repetition	REP

full form	abbreviation	full form	abbreviation
repetitive strain injury	RSI	resolution	RES
repetitive stress injury	RSI	rest and recreation; rest and relaxation	RANDR
reply	ANS	rest in peace	RIP
report	REPT; RPT	restricted	R
report program generator	RPG	résumé	CV
representative	AM; MEP; MHR; MP; MSP; REP; TD	resuscitation	CPR
		Retail Motor Industry Federation	RMI
reprint; reprinted	REPR	retail price index	RPI
reprobate	REP	retail price maintenance	RPM
republic	R; REP	retain	RET
Republican	REP	retinitis pigmentosa	RP
Republicans	GOP; IRA	retired	RET; RETD; RTD
reputation	REP	retroviruses	ERV
resale price maintenance	RPM	return	RET
		return to the beginning	DC
rescue service	AA; RAC	return to the sign	DS
research	RES	returned	RETD
research department explosive	RDX	returned letter office	RLO
research place	LAB	Returned Services Association	RSA
research programme	ESPRIT	Returned Services League	RSL
researchers	ACER; AERE; AHRB; ARA; CERN; ESRO; ESTEC; MHRA; MORI; NOP; OR	Revelation of St John	REV
		Reverend	REV; REVD
		reverse Polish notation	RPN
reservation	RES; REZ	revise; revised	REV
reserve	RES	Revised Standard Version	RSV
reserve decoration	RD	Revised Version	REVVER; RV
reservists	RNR; RNVR; TA	revision	REV
residence	RES	revolutions per minute	RPM
resident magistrate	RM	revolutions per second	RPS
resident medical officer	RMO	Rex	R
residual current device	RCD	rhenium	RE
resin	PVA	rheostat	POT
resistance	R	rhesus	RH
resistant bacterium	MRSA		

full form	abbreviation	full form	abbreviation
Rhesus factor	RH	Romania	R; RO
rhetoric	RHET	Romans	ROM
rheumatoid arthritis	RA	Romeo	R
Rhode Island	RI	Röntgen unit	R
rhodium	RH	rook	R
ribonucleic acid(s)	RNA	room	RM
rich text format	RTF	Roosevelt	FDR
rider	PS	root	R
rifle association	NRA; NSRA	root mean square	RMS
Rifle Brigade	RB	Rosalind; Rosamond; Rosamund	ROS; ROZ
right	OK; R; RT		
right hand	RH	rotten	NG
Right Honourable	RTHON	rouble(s)	R
Right Reverend	RR; RTREV	roughly	*see* about
Right Worshipful	RW	round	O
Right Worthy	RW	rowers	ARA; FISA
right-hand page	RO	royal	*see* monarch
ring	O	Royal Academician	RA
ritenuto	RIT	Royal Academy (of Arts)	RA
river	R	Royal Academy of Dramatic Art	RADA
river authority	PLA		
rivers authority	NRA	Royal Academy of Music	RAM
road	A; AB; A1; A1M; B; M; M1; RD; *see also* street		
		Royal Air Force	RAF
		Royal and Ancient	RA
		Royal Artillery	RA
road traffic accident	RTA	Royal Association for Disability and Rehabilitation	RADAR
Robert	BOB; DOB; R; RAB; ROB		
robot	BOT	Royal Australian Navy	RAN
rocket	SAM; V1	Royal Canadian Academy	RCA
Roderick; Rodney	ROD		
roger	OK	Royal Canadian Air Force	RCAF
role-playing game	RPG		
roller	RR	Royal Canadian Navy	RCN
Rolls-Royce®	RR	Royal College of Art	RCA
roman	RC; ROM	Royal Economic Society	RES
Roman Catholic	RC		
Roman Catholic Church	RCC	Royal Engineers	RE
		Royal Highness	RH

full form ⇨ abbreviation

Royal Horse Artillery	RHA	run	R
Royal Institution	RI	run batted in	RBI
Royal Mail	RM	run out	RO
Royal Marines	RM	runner	R
Royal Navy	RN	runs	R
Royal Society	RS	rupee	MR; R; RE
royalty	*see* monarch	rupees	R; RS
rubidium	RB	rural dean	RD
ruble(s)	*see* rouble(s)	rural development council	RDC
rudiments	ABC	Russell	AE
rugby	RL; RU	Russia	RUS
rugby footballers	RFC; RFU	ruthenium	RU
Rugby League	RL	rutherford	RD
Rugby Union	RU	rutherfordium	RF
rule	R	Rwanda	RWA
ruler	*see* monarch		

Sabbath	S; SUN	satellite information services	SIS
saboteur	SAB	satisfactory	OK
sadomasochism	SM	Saturday	SAT
sadomasochistic	SANDM	sauce	HP
safe working load	SWL	saucer	UFO
safety council	NSC	Saudi Arabia	SA
safety mark	CE	save	SA
sailed	SLD	save as you earn	SAYE
sailor	AB; OS; PO; TAR	Save the Children Fund	SCF
sailors	MN; RAN; RFA; RN; RYA; RYS	savings account	ISA; TESSA
saint	S; ST	savings and loan; savings and loan association	SANDL
Sainte	STE		
saints	SS	savings scheme	ISA; PEP; TESSA
sale or return	SOR	say	EG; ZB
salesman; saleswoman	REP	scan	CAT; CT; MRI; PET
salt	AB; NACL; OS; TAR	Scandinavian	SCAN; SCAND
Salvation Army	SA	scandium	SC
samarium	SM	scanner	CAT; CT; PET; SPET
the same	DO; ID	Scarlatti's works	K
the same as	IQ	schilling	S; SCH
Samoa	WS	scholar	BA; L; MA; see also Appendix: Degrees
Samuel	SAM		
San Marino	RSM		
sanatorium	SAN	scholastic aptitude test	SAT
sanctimonious	PI	school	BARTS; BSM; GS; GSM; HS; LAMDA; LBS; LSE; RADA; RAM; RIAM; RMA; RMAS; RSA; RSAMD; RSM; SCH
sanction	OK		
Sandhurst	RMA; RMAS		
sandwich filling	BLT		
Sanskrit	SANS; SANSK; SKR; SKT		
São Tomé and Príncipe	ST		
sapper	RE; SPR	School Certificate	CSE; SC
sappers	RE	Schubert's works	D
Sara; Sarah	SAL	Schutzstaffel	SS
Saskatchewan	SK	science	SCI
satellite	DBS; ECS		

full form	abbreviation	full form	abbreviation
science fiction	SF	search and rescue	SAR
science foundation	NSF	search for extraterrestrial intelligence	SETI
scientific	SCI		
scientific system of units	SI	seasonal affective disorder	SAD
scientist	BESS; BS; BSC; MSC	secant	SEC
		second	B; MO; S; SEC
scientists	RCS	second character; second letter	B
scire facias	SCIFA		
score	XX	second sight	ESP
Scotland	SCOT	second thoughts	PS
Scotsman	M; MAC; MC	secondary	B
Scottish	SCOT	second-class	B
Scottish Arts Council	SAC	second-hand	SH
Scottish Executive Education Department	SEED	second-rate	B
		seconds	S
Scottish Premier League	SPL	secret	QT
		Secret Intelligence Service	SIS
Scottish Qualifications Authority	SQA		
		secretary	SEC; SECY
Scottish Trades Union Congress	STUC	section	S; SECT
		secure electronic transaction	SET
Scottish Women's Rural Institute	SWRI		
		secure sockets layer	SSL
scrape	DANDC	Securities and Exchange Commission	SEC
screed	MS		
screen	VDU	Securities and Futures Authority	SFA
screw steamer	SS		
scripture	NT; OT; RE; RI; SCRIPT	Securities and Investments Board	SIB
		security agency	FBI; FSB; MI; NSA; SIS
scruple	SCR		
sculpted: he/she sculpted	SC;		
		Security Intelligence Service	SIS
sculptor; sculpture	SCULP; SCULPT		
sea	MED	security service	*see* security agency
seaborgium	SG	see	C; V
sealed with a loving kiss	SWALK	selenium	SE
		self	I
seaman	*see* sailor	self-catering	SC
seamen	*see* sailors	self-contained	SC

full form ⇨ abbreviation

self-regulatory organization	SRO
seller's opinion	SO
semester	SEM
semicolon	SEM
seminary	SEM
Semitic	SEM
senate; senator	SEN
Senegal	SN
senior	SEN; SNR; SR
senior citizen	OAP
senior combination room; senior common room	SCR
senior executive officer	SEO
senior medical officer	SMO
senior nursing officer	SNO
Senior Service	RN
señor	SR
senza	SEN
separate	SEP
separationists; separatists	ETA
September	SEP; SEPT
Septuagint	LXX
Serbia and Montenegro	YU
sergeant	NCO; PS; SERG; SERGT; SERJ; SERJT; SGT; SL; SM; *see also* Appendix: Serviceman, Servicewoman
serjeant-at-law	SL
sergeant-major	NCO; SM
serial	SER
series	SER
serine	SER
Serious Fraud Office	SFO
serjeant	*see* sergeant

sermon	SER
serum	ATS
service	ATS; RAAF; RAF; RAN; RCAF; RCN; RN; RNZAF; RNZN; USAF; USN
serviceman; servicewoman	*see* Appendix: Serviceman, Servicewoman
servicemen; servicewomen	*see* Appendix: Armed Services
session	SESS
set of books	NT; OT
seven	S; VII
seventy	LXX; S
seventy thousand	S
sex appeal	SA
sexless	N
sexual practices	SANDM; SM
sexually transmitted disease	STD; VD
Seychelles	SY
sforzando	FZ; SF; SFZ
sforzato	SF; SFZ
shakes	DT; DTS
Shakespeare	WS
shall	LL
share	DIV; PIBS; SHR
share index	FTSE
share ownership plan	ESOP
share purchase	EXDIV
shares	SHR
Shaw	GBS
sheet	CEL; SHT
sheets	SHT
shilling	S
ship	HMAS; HMCS; HMS; MV; Q; SS; ULCC; USS

full form ⇨ abbreviation

shipment	SHPT	signed	SGD
shipping line	PANDO	significant other person	SOP
shipping order	SO		
ships	*see* navy	signor; signore	SIG
shire	*see* Appendix: Counties of England and Wales	silicon	SI
		silk	KC; QC
		silver	AG
shirt	T	Simeonite	SIM
shock treatment	ECT	Simon	SIM
shooters	NRA	simple harmonic motion	SHM
shop	*see* store		
shopworkers	USDAW	sine	SIN
short message service	SMS	sine die	SD
short metre	SM	Singapore	SGP
short time	MO; S; SEC	single	EP; 1
short wave	SW	Single European Act	SEA
shortage	SHTG	single transferable vote	STV
shorthand	SH	singular	S; SING
sibling	BRO; SIB; SIS	sinister	L; LH
sick building syndrome	SBS	Sinn Fein	SF
		sir	SR
side	11; L; R; XI; XV	sister	SIS; SR
sides	LR; RL	six	VI
siemens	S	Six Counties	NI
sierra	S	sixpence	VID; VIP
Sierra Leone	WAL	sixth sense	ESP
sievert(s)	SV	sixty	LX
sign	V	skiers	FIS
sign of love	X	sleep	REM; ZZ
sign of the times	X	Slovakia	SK
signal	SOS	Slovenia	SLO
Signal Corps	RCS; SC	slowing gradually	RALL; RIT
signal frequency	SF	smacker	X
signal officer	SO	small	S
signal passed at danger	SPAD	small businesses	FSB
signallers	RCS; SC	small capitals	SC
signalling and telecommunications	SANDT	small change	P
		small letters	LC
signature	SIG	small measure	CC; MIL; OZ

small number	I; II; III; IV; IX; V; VI; VII; VIII
small office/home office	SOHO
small quantity	CC
small women; small women's	SW
smallest room	*see* toilet
smell	BO
Smith	FE
smokers	FOREST
snap; snapshot	PIC
snore	ZZ
snoring	ZZ
soap	ER
sober	TT
social, domestic and pleasure	SDP
social worker	MSW; PSW
social workers	BASW
socialist	SOC
Socialists	LAB; LP; PASOK; PLP; SDLP; SDP; SWP
socially acceptable	U
society	BCS; BS; CMS; EDS; EETS; ISBA; LS; NAS; NES; PRS; PS; RES; RSC; RSL; RS; S; SA; SOC; SSC; TOCH; U
Society of Antiquaries	SA
Society of Arts	SA
Society of the Holy Cross	SSC
sodium	NA
soft	B; P
soldier	GI; *see also* Appendix: Serviceman, Servicewoman

soldiers	ATS; BEF; HA; LI; OR; RA; RB; RE; RHA; SAS; TA; UDR; *see also* Appendix: Armed Services
solicitor	ATT; SL; SOL; SOLR
solicitor at law	SL
Solicitor before the Supreme Courts	SSC
Solicitor-General	SG; SOLGEN
Solomon	SOL
solution	ANS; AQ; SOL
solvent	DMSO
Somalia	SO
somebody	VIP
Somerset	SOM
son	S
Song of Solomon	SOFS
Song of Songs	SOFS
sons	S
soprano	S; SOP
soprano, alto, tenor, bass	SATB
sound effects	FX
south	S; SO; STH
South Africa	RSA; SA; SAFR; ZA
South African	SAFR
South America	SA
South Australia	SA
South Carolina	SC
South Dakota	SD; SDAK
South Island	SI
South Korea	ROK
south-east	SE
South-East Asia Command	SEAC
south-eastern	SE

southern	S
Southern Region	SR
south-south-east	SSE
south-south-west	SSW
south-west	SW
South-West Africa	SWA
south-western	SW
sovereign	L; SOV; *see also* monarch
Soviet Ministry of Internal Affairs	MVD
Soviet secret police	KGB
Soviet Socialist Republic	SSR
space walk	EVA
spacecraft	LEM
spades	S
Spain	E
spangle	O
Spanish company	CIA
speaks	LOQ
special	S; SP
Special Air Service	SAS
special area of conservation	SAC
Special Boat Service	SBS
special constable	SC
special drawing rights	SDR; SDRS
special education needs	SEN
special effects	FX; SFX
special government political administration	OGPU
special interest group	SIG
Special Operations Executive	SOE
special order	SO
special patrol group	SPG
special protection area	SPA

Special Temporary Employment Programme	STEP
special weapons and tactics	SWAT
species	SP; SPP
specific	SPECIF
specific gravity	SG; SPGR
specific latent heat per gramme	L
specific volume	SPVOL
specifically	SPECIF
spectacles	OO
speech therapist	LCST
speed	MPH; V
speed of light	C
spelling	SP
spelling-book	ABC
Spenser	ED
spies	CIA; MI
spooks	CIA
sport	RL; RU
sport utility vehicle	SUV
spymaster	M
squadron	SQN
square	S; SQ; T
Sri Lanka	CL
St Albans: of St Albans	ALBAN
St Lucia	WL
St Vincent and the Grenadines	WV
staff association	APEX
staff officer	SO
Staffordshire	STAFFS
stamped addressed envelope	SAE
standard	STD
standard assessment task	SAT
standard book number	SBN

standard serial number	SSN	store	BHS; DRAM; EDORAM; EEPROM; EPROM; EROM; GUM; IAS; MANDS; PROM; PX; SRAM
standard spending assessment	SSA		
standard temperature and pressure	STP		
standard wire gauge	SWG		
stand-in	SUB	storm section	SA
standing order	SO	storm troopers	SA
standing room only	SRO	stove	AGA
Star Wars	SDI	straight	HET; STR
starboard	R	strait	ST
start of year	JAN	strangeness	S
starting price	SP	Strategic Air Command	SAC
state	*see* Appendix: US States	Strategic Arms Limitation Talks; Strategic Arms Limitation Treaty	SALT
states	US; USA		
station	STA		
statutory sick pay	SSP	Strategic Arms Reduction Talks; Strategic Arms Reduction Treaty	START
stay-on-tab	SOT		
stealing a car	TWOC		
steamer	SS; STR		
steamship	SS	Strategic Defense Initiative	SDI
steradian	SR		
sterling	LSD; STER; STG	Strategic Health Authority	SHA
Stevenson	RLS		
stimulant	DEX; E; MDMA; PH	Strategic Rail Authority	SRA
		strategic services office	OSS
stimulation	TENS; TMS	street	AV; AVE; BLVD; CLO; CRES; DR; DV; GDNS; GRO; LA; PK; PL; RD; ST; TER; TERR; WY
Stock Exchange Automated Quotations	SEAQ		
Stock Exchange Electronic Trading Service	SETS		
		street map	AZ
stokes	S	strengths, weaknesses, opportunities and threats	SWOT
stolid	PO		
stone	ST		
		stress	RSI
		string	G
		strong	F; STR

full form ⇨ abbreviation

strontium	SR	sunlight	UV
student	L	super	A1; FAB
Student Christian Movement	SCM	super video graphics array	SVGA
student of civil law	SCL	superb	A1; FAB
Student Representative Council	SRC	superbug	MRSA; SARS
students	NUS	superfine	SUP
stumped	ST	superhigh frequency	SHF
stun; stunner	KO	superintendent	SUPT
subaltern	SUB	superior	SUP; U
subeditor	SUB	superior court	SUPCT
subject	PE; RE; RI; SUB SUBJ	superlative	SUP
		supersonic transport	SST
subject to contract	STC	supine	SUP
subjective	SUBJ	supplement	PS; SUP; SUPP; SUPPL; TES; TLS
subjunctive	SUBJ		
sublieutenant	SUB	support; supporter	BRA
submarine	SUB	supreme	SUP; SUPR
subscriber	SUB	supreme court	SUPCT
subscriber trunk dialling	STD	Supreme Judicial Court	SJC
subscription	SUB; SUBS	sure	OK
subsistence money	SUB	surface acoustic wave	SAW
subspecies	SSP; SSPP	surface tension	T
substantive	SB; SUBST	surface-mounted device	SMD
substitute	SUB; SUBST	surfeit	OD
succeeded	S	surgeon	BCH; BS; CH; CHB; CHM; CM; DCH; DS; FRCS; LCH; LCHIR; LRCS; MCH; MS; SURG
Sudan	SUD		
sufficient quantity	QS		
suffix	SFX		
suit	G		
suitable for children	U	surgeons	RCS
sulphur	S	surgery; surgical	OP; SURG
summary	SYNOP	Suriname	SME
summertime	BST	Surrey	SY
sun	S	surveyor	CS
sun protection factor	SPF	surveyors	RICS
Sunday	S; SUN		

full form ⇨ abbreviation

S

Susan; Susanna; Susannah; Susanne; Suzanna; Suzannah; Suzanne	SUE; SUS	synonym	SYN
		synthetic	SYN
		Syria	SYR
Swaziland	SD	system	ABS; ACS; AMCS; ANS; AWACS; BACS; BBS; CBIS; CHAPS; CNS; CPM; DDE; DNS; DOS; DBMS; DMS; EMS; GCA; GIS; GRACE; GSM; IAS; ILS; LETS; MIDAS; MSDOS®; NWS; OMOV; POTS; PSS; QADS; RDS; SARSAT; SI; UMTS
Sweden	S		
sweet	PUD		
sweet Fanny Adams	SFA		
sweetheart	HON		
sweetly	DOL		
swimmers	ASA; FINA		
Switzerland	CH		
syllable	SYL		
syllabus	SYL		
symbol	SYM		
symmetrical	SYM		
sympathetic treatment	TLC	system of radar stations	NWS
symphony	SYM	system of transferring money	BACS; CHAPS;
symptom	SYM		
syndicate	SYND		
syndrome	AIDS; CFS; CTS; FAS; IBS; ME; MFS; PMS; PVFS; PWS; SBS; SIDS; SUDS; TSS		

tablespoon; tablespoonful	TBSP	Teaching English as a Second Language	TESL
tablet	E; TAB	Teaching English to Speakers of Other Languages	TESOL
tabulate; tabulator	TAB		
Taiwan	RC	team	11; XI; XV
Tajikistan	TJ	teaspoon; teaspoonful	TSP
take	R; REC		
take notice	NB	technetium	TC
taking without owner's consent	TWOC	technical	TECH
		technical and further education	TAFE
Talbot House	TOCH		
tangent	TAN	technical drawing	TD
tango	T	technical knockout	TKO
tanker	ULCC	technology	TECH
tantalum	TA	tee	T
Tanzania	EAT	teetotal; teetotallers	TT
tap	C; H	telecommunications office	OFTEL
tape	DAT		
tar	*see* sailor	telegraph office	TO
tare	T	telepathy	ESP
tarpaulin	*see* sailor	telephone	TEL
Tasmania	TAS	telephone company	BT; ITT
tavern	PH	telephone exchange	PABX; PAX; PBX; PMBX; RAX
tax	CGT; CRT; CTT; GST; IHT; PRT; PT; VAT		
		telephone network	PCN; PSTN
		telephone number	TEL
tax and prices index	TPI	telephone service	ADC
tax collectors	IR; IRS	telephone system	GRACE; GSM; POTS; STD
tax officer	TO		
taxmen	IR; IRS	teleprinter	TPR
teacher	AST; BED	television	CCTV; HDTV; MTV; TV
teachers	ATL; AUT; NAHT; NUT; PAT		
		television audience measurement	TAM
teaching council	GTC; GTCE; GTCNI; GTCS; GTCW		
		tellurium	TE
		temperature	T; TEMP
teaching English	ELT	temperature-humidity index	THI
Teaching English as a Foreign Language	TEFL		
		temporal	TEMP
		temporary	TEMP

full form ⇨ abbreviation

ten	10; X	*The Chambers Dictionary*	TCD
ten thousand	X	the court wishes to be advised	CAV
tender loving care	TLC	theatre; theatrical	NT; REP; THEAT
Tennessee	TENN; TN	Their Royal Highnesses	TRH
tennis club	AELTC	them	EM
tenor	T	Theodore	TED
tense	T	theologian	BD; DD; DTH; DTHEOL; LTH; STP; THD; THEOL
tension	HT; LT; PMT; T		
tenuto	TEN		
terabyte(s)	TB		
terbium	TB	theological; theology	THEOL
term	SEM	theology professor	STP
terminate and stay resident	TSR	theory of everything	TOE
terrace	TER; TERR	therapist	LCST; OT; ROT; SLT
terriers; Territorial Army	TA	therapy	CST; DOTS; ECT; EST; HRT; ORT; OT; PT
Territorial Decoration	TD		
Territorials	TA		
Territory	TER; TERR	there is no alternative	TINA
terrorists	ETA; GRAPO; IRA; SA	thermoplastic	PET
		these days	AD
tesla	T	thesis	DISS
test	MOT	Thessalonians	THESS
testament	TEST	they did it; they made it	FF
Teutonic	TEUT		
Texas	TEX; TX	third-generation communications mobile system	UMTS
textured soya protein	TSP		
Thailand	T		
thallium	TL	third-rate	C
that	YT	third thoughts	PPS
that is	DH; IE; SC	thirty	XXX
that is to say	IE; SC	this era	AD
that's	IE	this month	CUR; CURT; INST
the	T		
the accused being absent	ABSERE; ABSRE	Thomas	TAM; TOM
		thorium	TH
the Bard	WS	thoroughfare	*see* road *and* street
		thou; thousand	G; K; M

95

full form	abbreviation	full form	abbreviation
three	III	toilet	APC; LAT; LAV; LOO; WC
three feet	Y; YD	tomography	PET
three hundred	B	ton	C; T
three thousand	B	Tonga	TON
three times a day	TID	tonne(s)	T
three-letter acronym	TLA	tons	T
through the lens	TTL	too much	OTT
through the rectum	PR	top brass	CIC; CINC; VIPS
thulium	TM	top class	A1; U
Thursday	TH; THU; THUR; THURS	top quality	A1
ticket	APEX	top-hole; top-notch	A1
time	D; H; HR; MIN; MO; SEC; T; WK; YR	torpedo boat	TB
		Tory	C
times	X	Totalizator Agency Board	TAB
Timothy	TIM	touching	RE
tin	SN	tourist board	ETB
tiro	L	Tourist Trophy	TT
titanium	TI	towards the end	ADFIN
title	DR; MR; MRS; MS; U	town planners	RTPI
		town sub-office	TSO
Titus	TIT	township	TP
to	T	tracks	*see* railway
to be advised	TBA	tractor	CAT
to be confirmed	TBC	trade agreement	GATT; NAFTA
to God, the best, the greatest	DOM	trade union	CGT; TU
		trademark	R
to infinity	ADINF	tradename	TN
to take leave	PPC	trader	ARB
to the beginning	ADINIT; DC	traders	EFTA
to the end	ADFIN	Trades Union Congress	TUC
to the greater glory of God	AMDG	trading service	SETS
to the sign	DS	trading system	LETS
to wit	SC; SCIL; SCIZ; VIZ	traditional Chinese medicine	TCM
Tobit	TOB	traditional Indian medicine	TIM
Togo	TG		

full form ⇨ abbreviation

train	APT; HST; TGV	treat with contempt	DIS
train operating company	TOC	treatise	DISS
trainee	L	treaty organization	SEATO
trainers	ATC; GTC	tricarboxylic acid cycle	TCA
training	PE; PT	trichosanthin	Q
Training and Enterprise Council	TEC	trick	CON
		Trinidad and Tobago	TT
trains	*see* railway	trinity	TRIN
transactions	TR	Trinity College, Dublin	TCD
transatlantic	US		
transcendental meditation	TM	Trinity College of Music, London	TCM
transfer	TRANSF	tripod	POD
transformational grammar	TG	tritium	T
		troop	TP
transient ischaemic attack	TIA	trooper	TPR
		troops	*see* soldiers
transitive	T; TR; TRANS	troy	T
translated; translation	TRANS	truck	PU; UTE
translator	TR	trunk	*see* main road
transmission control protocol	TCP	trust	AMEX; NT
		trusted third party	TTP
transmission electron microscope	TEM	trustee	TR
		tube	TV; U
transmitted by an amateur operator	CQ	tuberculin tested	TT
		tuberculosis	TB
transport officer	TO	tuberculosis treatment	DOTS
transport organization	BR; CIE; TIR	Tuesday	TU; TUE; TUES
Transport Organization of Ireland	CIE	tumour necrosis factor	TNF
		tungsten	W
transport system	RY	Tunisia	TN
transporters	RCT	tuppence	DD; PP
transpose	TR	Turkey	TR
trap	U	Turkmenistan	TM
travel agents	ABTA	turn	REV; U; UEY
traveller; travelling salesman	REP	turn over	PTO; TO
		turner	RPT
treasurer	CE; TREAS	tuxedo	DJ; TUX

twelve	DOZ; DZ; N; XII	two pence	DD; PP
twenty	XX	two shillings	FL
two	II	two thousand	Z
two hundred	H	Tyneside	NE
two hundred and fifty	E; K	type	BF
two hundred and fifty thousand	E	typographer; typography	TYP; TYPO
two hundred thousand	H	tyro	L
two million	Z	tyrosine	TYR

U

U-boat	SUB	under-secretary	US
Uganda	EAU	underwear	BRA
Ukraine	UA	underwrite	PS
Ulster	NI	unidentified	INCOG
Ulster Defence Association	UDA	unidentified flying object	UFO
Ulster Defence Regiment	UDR	uniform	U
Ulster Freedom Fighters	UFF	uniform business rate	UBR
		uniform resource locator	URL
Ulster Unionist	UU	uninterruptible power supply	UPS
ultimate; ultimately	ULT	union	U; *see also* Appendix: Unions
ultimo	ULT		
ultra-heat treated	UHT	unionist	U
ultra-high frequency	UHF	unionists	AU; DUP; EOKA; OAU; UU
ultra-high temperature	UHT		
ultra-large crude carrier	ULCC	unique selling point; unique selling proposition	USP
ultra-low frequency	ULF		
ultrashort waves	USW	unit	A; ALU; AMU; AU; AWU; BQ; BTU; C; CCU; CD; CPU; EMU; ESU; ETSU; F; GAL; GEV; GY; H; HZ; 1; ICU; J; K; KAT; KG; KWH; LM; LX; M; MKSA; MOL; N; OCTU; P; PA; PT; R; RA; RAD; S; SR; SV; T; TA; V; VDU; W
ultrasonic waves	USW		
ultraviolet	UV		
ultraviolet radiation	UVA; UVB; UVC; UVR		
ultra-wideband	UWB		
umpire	REF; UMP		
unaccounted for	AWOL; MIA		
unanimous	NEMCON; NEMDISS		
uncle	SAM		
Uncle Sam	US; USA		
uncommitted logic array	ULA	Unitarian	UNIT
		united	U; UTD
undated	ND; SA; SD	United Arab Emirates	UAE
under an assumed name	INCOG	United Arab Republic	UAR
		United Democratic Front	UDF
under that heading	SV		
under the voice	SV	United Dominions Trust	UDT
under the word	SV		
undergraduate	L	United Free Church	UF

U

full form ⇨ abbreviation

United Kingdom	GB; UK	university	ANU; MIT; NUI; OU; U; UMIST; UNI; UNIV; UWIST
United Nations	UN		
United Nations Association	UNA		
United Nations Children's Fund	UNICEF	University College	UC
		unknown	IGN; INCOG; X; Y; Z
United Nations Organization	UNO	unknown number; unlimited number	N
United Presbyterian	UP		
United Reformed Church	URC	unlisted securities market	USM
United Service	US	unnamed	ANON
United Service Organizations	USO	unpaid	HON
		unserviceable	US
United Services	US	unsexed; unsexy	N
United States; United States of America	US; USA	upper case	CAPS; UC
		upper class	U
unity	1	upper house	HL
universal	U	uppish	U
Universal Decimal Classification	UDC	upright	PI
		uranium	U
Unilateral Declaration of Human Rights	UDHR	uranium hexafluoride	HEX
		urgent appeal	SOS
Universal Declaration of Independence	UDI	Uruguay	ROU; U; URU
		us	S
Universal Time	UT	used	SH
Universal Time Co-ordinated	UTC	useless	US
		usually	USU
Universalist	U	Utah	UT
Universities and Colleges Admissions Service	UCAS	utility truck; utility vehicle	UTE
		U-turn	UEY
Universities Central Council on Admissions	UCCA	Uzbekistan	UZ
Universities Funding Council	UFC		

vacation	HOL; HOLS; VAC	vertical motion index	VMI
vaccination	BCG; DPT; MMR	very	V
vaccine	BCG; DPT; MMR; TAB	very black	BB
		very good	VG
valentine	VAL	very hard	HH
Valerie	VAL	very high frequency	VHF
value for money	VFM	very important person	VIP
value-added reseller	VAR	very large	OS; XL
value-added tax	VAT	very loud	FF
vanadium	V	very quiet	PP
Vancouver Island	VI	Very Reverend	VREV
vanguard	VAN	very soft	BB; PP
variable	VAR; X; Y; Z	very well indeed	OPT
variant	VAR	Very Worshipful	VW
variant reading	VARLECT; VL; VR	vessel	*see* boat *and* ship
variety	VAR	veteran	VET
Vatican; Vatican City	V	veterans	BL; GAR
vatu	V; VT	Veterinary Surgeon	VET; VETSURG; VS
vee	V	veterinary surgeons	RAVC; RCVS
vegetable; vegetables	VEG	vicar	REV
vegetate	VEG	Vicar Apostolic	VA
Vehicle Inspectorate	VI	Vicar General	VG
vehicle test	MOT	vicarage	VIC
velocity	V	vice versa	VV
velocity constant	K	vice-admiral	VA
venerable	VEN	vice-chancellor	VC; VICE
venereal disease	NSU; STD; VD	vice-president	VICE; VP
Venezuela	YV	Victor	V; VIC
venture capital trust	VCT	Victoria	VIC; VIR; VR; VRI
verb	V; VB		
verb intransitive	VI	Victoria and Albert	VA
verb transitive	VT	Victoria Cross	VC
Vermont	VT	Victoria, Empress and Queen	VIR
vermouth	IT		
verse	V	Victoria, Queen and Empress	VRI
verses	VV		
verso	V; VO	victory	V; VE; VJ
versus	V; VS	vide	V

full form	abbreviation	full form	abbreviation
video	VID	viz	SC
Video Electronics Standards Association	VESA	vocabulary	VOCAB
		vocative	VOC
video frequency	VF	voice frequency	VF
video graphics array	VGA	Voice of America	VOA
video jockey	VJ	Volkswagen	VW
video-on-demand	VOD	volt(s)	V
Vietnam	NAM; VN	volume	CC; TOM; V; VOL
view	VW	volumes	VV
village	VIL; VILL	voluntary	VOL
Violet	VI	Voluntary Aid Detachment	VAD
Virgin Islands	VI	volunteer	CSV; VOL
Virginia	VA	volunteer nurses	VAD
virtual reality	VR	volunteers	CDV; TA
virus	CDV; CMV; EB; EBV; HIV; HPV; HTLV; SARS	vote	X
		voting system	OMOV; PR
viscount	VIS; VISC	vulgar	VULG
visible panty line	VPL	Vulgate	VUL; VULG
visual display unit	VDU	Vyvian; Vyvyan	VYV
vitamin	A; B; C; D; E; K		
Vivian; Vivien; Vivyan	VIV		

waiting on weather	WOW	week	W; WK
walk	EVA	weekly	TES; TLS
walkover	WO	weeks	*see* month
wall	WA	weight	AGW; CG; CT; CWT; DG; G; GM; GR; GRT; GVW; GW; HG; K; KG; L; LB; MG; OZ; ST; W; WT
Walloon	WAL		
WAP Internet service provider	WISP		
War Office	WO		
warplane	EFA; F; MIG; MRCA	Welsh	CYM; W
		Welshman	DAI
Warrant Officer	WO	Wesley	WES
Warsaw Pact	WP	west	W
Warwickshire	WAR	West Africa	WA
Washington	DC; WA; WASH	West Central	WC
wastepaper basket	WPB	West End	WC; W1
watchdog	CA	West Indies	WI
water	AQ	West Virginia	WV
water closet	WC	western	W
water colourist(s)	RI	Western Australia	WA
water gauge	WG	Western European Time	WET
waterproof	MAC		
watt	W	Western European Union	WEU
way	E; MO; N; S; W; WY; *see also* road *and* street		
		Western Region	WR
		Western Samoa	WS
way of working	MO	Westminster	HP; SW1
weak	PP; W	west-north-west	WNW
weakly interacting massive particles	WIMP	west-south-west	WSW
		wheel-drive	WD
weapon	AAM; ABM; AGM; ALCM; AMRAAM; ASBM; ASM; ATM; GAT; ICBM; IRBM; MG; MRBM; SAM; SLBM; SLR; SSM; STEN; TASM; V1	which see	QQV; QV
		which was to be done	QEF
		which was to be found	QEI
		which was to be proved	QED
		whiskey	W
		whistle-blower	REF
		white	W
weather permitting	WP	Whitehall warriors	MOD
weber	WB	whore	PRO
Wednesday	WED; WEDS		

wicket	W	Women and the Church	WATCH
wide	W	women's	W
wide area information server; wide area information servers	WAIS	Women's Institute(s)	WI
		won	W
wide area network	WAN	wonderful	A1; FAB
width	W	Worcester: of Worcester	WIGORN
wife	MRS; UX; W	Worcestershire	WORCS
will	LL	word processing; word processor	WP
William	WM		
Wiltshire	WILTS	words per minute	WPM
Winchester: of Winchester	WINTON	work	OP; WK
		workers	TU; TUC
windows, icons, mouse and pointer	WIMP	Workers' Educational Association	WEA
wine	IT	works by Bach	BWV
Winifred	WIN	works by Beethoven	WOO
wire gauge	WG	works by Mozart	K
Wireless Application Protocol	WAP	works by Scarlatti	K
		works by Schubert	D
Wisconsin	WI; WIS; WISC	Works Department	WD
Wisdom	SIR	World Chess Federation	FIDE
with	W		
with effect from	WEF	World Health Organization	WHO
with increasing speed	ACCEL		
with regard to; with respect to	RE; WRT	World Tourism Organization	WTO
		World Trade Organization	WTO
with sudden emphasis	SF; SFZ		
without	WO; X	world wide web	WWW
without a day	SD	Worship	WP
without charge	WC	Worshipful	WP; WPFL
without children	SP	would	D
without date	SA; SD	wouldst	DST
without issue	SP	writ	SCIFA
wolfram	W	write once read many times	WORM
woman	F; *see also* Appendix: First Names		
		Writer to the Signet	WS
women	W	writers	PEN

full form ⇨ abbreviation

Writers and Artists Guild	WAG	wrong fount	WF
writing	MS; R	wye	Y
wrong	X	Wyoming	WY; WYO

xenon	XE	Youth Training Scheme	YTS
Xmas	XM	ytterbium	YB
		yttrium	Y
yacht	MY	Yugoslavia	YU; YUG
Yankee	Y	Yukon Territory	YT
yard	Y; YD		
yards	YD; YDS	Zaire	ZRE
year	A; Y; YR	Zambia	Z
year to date	YTD	Zechariah	ZECH
yearly	PA	zed; zee	Z
yearly meeting	AGM	zenith	Z
years	YRS	Zephaniah	ZEP
Yemen	YAR	zero	FA; O; SFA; Z
yen	Y; YN	zero-emission vehicle	ZEV
yeomanry	YEO	zero-energy thermonuclear apparatus	ZETA
yes	OK		
York	EBOR	zilch	FA; O; SFA
York: of York	EBOR	Zimbabwe	ZW
Yorkshire	YORKS	zinc	ZN
young	Y	zip	FA; O; SFA; *see also* Appendix: US States
Young Conservative(s)	YC		
younger	YR	zirconium	ZR
your	YR	zloty	ZL
Your Holiness	SV	zone	Z
yours	YRS	Zone Standard Time	ZST
yours truly	I	zoologist	FZS
youth	MOD; TED	zoologists	RZS; RZSE
Youth Hostels Association	YHA	Zulu	Z
Youth Opportunities Programme	YOP		

NUMBERS

0	O	400	CD; G; P
1	A; I; J	500	A; D; Q
2	II	501	DI
3	III	505	DV
4	IV	510	DX
5	V	550	DL
6	VI	600	DC
7	S; VII	900	CM
8	VIII	1,000	G; K; M
9	IX	£1,000; $1,000	G
10	X	1,001	MI
11	O; XI	1,005	MV
12	DOZ; DZ; XII	1,010	MX
15	XV	1,050	ML
20	XX	1,100	MC
30	XXX	1,500	MD
40	F; XL	2,000	MM; Z
49	IL	3,000	B
50	A; L	5,000	A; V
51	LI	10,000	X
55	LV	11,000	O
60	LX	40,000	F
70	LXX; S	50,000	L
80	LXXX; R	70,000	S
90	N; XC	80,000	R
99	IC	90,000	N
100; $100	C	150,000	Y
101	CI	160,000	T
105	CV	200,000	H
110	CX	250,000	E; K
150	CL; Y	400,000	G; P
160	CLX; T	500,000	D; Q
200	CC; H	1,000,000	M
250	CCL; E; K	2,000,000	Z
300	CCC; B		

PART TWO

ABBREVIATION ⇨ FULL FORM

A	about; absent; absolute; academician; academy; acceleration; accepted; ace; acre; acreage; acres; across; acting; active; adjective; adult; advance; advanced; afternoon; all; alpha; alto; amateur; America; American; ammeter; ampere; Ångström; anonymous; answer; ante; anterior; approximately; are; area; argon; around; article; associate; athletic; atomic; atomic weight; Australia; Australian; Austria; before; blood group; classification; examination; fifty; film classification; first; first character; first letter; first-class; first-rate; five hundred; five thousand; high-class; Honour; 1; in equal quantities of each; in the year; key; level; note; one; road; unit; vitamin; year; 50; 500; 5,000	AAC	army; Army Air Corps; athletes; club
		AAM	missile; weapon
		AAP	press
		AAR	against all risks; average annual rainfall
		AASIA	Australasia
		AAT	protein
		AB	abdominal muscle; Advisory Board; airborne; Alberta; autobahn; Bachelor of Arts; blood group; blue jacket; degree; motorway; muscle; road; sailor; salt
		ABA	barristers; boxers
		ABB	abbess; abbey; abbot
		ABBR; ABBREV	abbreviated; abbreviation
		ABC	Arab Banking Corporation; Associated British Cinemas; Audit Bureau of Circulations; broadcasters; company; network; reader; rudiments; spelling-book
		ABD	abdicated; abridged
AA	abstainers; ack-ack; Alcoholics Anonymous; anti-aircraft; architects; Architectural Association; army; Associate of Arts; Australian Army; Automobile Association; classification; club; drivers; driving club; film classification; flak; former drinkers; in equal quantities of each; motorists	ABE	Abraham; Lincoln
		ABER	Aberdeen
		ABF	Actors' Benevolent Fund; Army Benevolent Fund
		ABH	actual bodily harm
		ABI	insurers
		ABINIT	from the beginning
		ABL	ablative; case
		ABM	missile; weapon
		ABP	archbishop; clergyman; clergywoman
AAA	anti-aircraft artillery; athletes; drivers; motorists	ABR	abridged; abridgement
		ABRSM	examiners; musicians

ABS	absence; absent; absolute; absolutely; absorbent; abstract; braking system; system	**ACE**	Advisory Centre for Education; Allied Command Europe; arts council; conservationists; preservationists
ABSERE	in the absence of the accused; the accused being absent	**ACER**	researchers
		ACGB	arts council
ABSOL	absolute; absolutely	**ACIB**	banker
ABSRE	in the absence of the accused; the accused being absent	**ACII**	insurer
		ACL	anterior cruciate ligament; ligament
ABSTR	abstract	**ACM**	air-chief-marshal
ABTA	travel agents	**ACMA**	manager
AC	account; account current; acre; across; actinium; Aero Club; Air Corps; air-conditioned; air-conditioning; aircraftman; aircraftsman; airman; Alpine Club; alternating current; appellation contrôlée; appellation d'origine contrôlée; athletes; athletic club; before Christ; before food; bill; club; companion; current	**ACNI**	arts council
		ACORN®	Classification of Residential Neighbourhoods
		ACP	African, Caribbean and Pacific
		ACPO; ACPOS	police chiefs
		ACPT	acceptance
		ACRE	environmentalists
		ACS	active control system; system
		ACT	acting; active
ACA	accountant	**ACTG**	acting
ACAS	arbitrators; mediators; peacemaker(s)	**ACTH**	hormone
		ACW	aircraftswoman; aircraftwoman; arts council
ACC	acceptance; Accident Compensation Corporation; accompanied; according; account; accountant; accusative; case	**AD**	active duty; advantage; advertisement; after date; air defence; Alzheimer's disease; analogue-to-digital; anno Domini; announcement; before the day; bill; commercial; condition; contemporary; dame; illness; in the year of our Lord; in the year of the Lord; modern; notice; now; plug; poster; publicity; puff; these days
ACCA	accountant(s)		
ACCEL	accelerando; with increasing speed		
ACCT	account		
ACCUS	accusative; case		

ADA	enzyme	AE	account executive; aged; Air Efficiency Award; award; of her/his age; poet; Russell
ADC	advice of duration and charge; aide-de-camp; charge advice; telephone service		
		AEA	Atomic Energy Authority
ADD	addendum; addition; additional; address; illness	AEC	Atomic Energy Commission
		AEEU	engineers
ADF	automatic direction-finder	AELTC	club; croquet club; tennis club
ADFIN	at the end; to the end; towards the end	AER	annual equivalent rate; rate
ADH	hormone	AERE	researchers
ADHD	illness	AET	after extra time; aged; of her/his age
ADI	approved driving instructor, driving instructor	AEW	airborne early warning
		AF	admiral of the fleet; Anglo-French; associate fellow; audio-frequency
ADINF	ad infinitum; to infinity		
ADINIT	at the beginning; to the beginning	AFA	footballers
ADINT	for the meantime; in the meantime	AFC	Air Force Cross; automatic flight control; club; football club
ADJ	adjective; adjourned; adjustment; adjutant		
		AFG	Afghanistan
ADJT	adjutant	AFM	Air Force Medal; audio-frequency modulation
ADL	Activity of Daily Living		
ADLIB	at pleasure; at will; extempore; extemporize; impromptu; make up	AFP	press agency; protein
		AFR	Africa; African
		AFV	armoured fighting vehicle
ADLOC	at the place	AG	adjutant-general; Attorney-General; company; joint stock company; silver
ADM	admiral		
ADMIN	administration		
ADP	automatic data processing; information technology		
		AGA	air-ground-air; oven
		AGC	automatic gain control
ADV	advent; adverb; advisory; advocate; against	AGM	meeting; missile; weapon
		AGR	advanced gas-cooled reactor; agriculture; reactor
ADVAL	to value		
ADVT	advertisement, bill, plug, poster; publicity		
		AGRIC	agriculture
		AGT	advanced gas turbine; agent; agreement

AGW	actual gross weight; weight	AL	Alabama; Albania; Albert; aluminium; Anglo-Latin; Capone; gangster
AH	ampere hour; in the year of Hegira		
AHA	acid	ALA	acid; Alabama; librarian
AHL	at this place; here	ALAS	Alaska
AHQ	Allied Headquarters; army headquarters	ALB	Albania
		ALBAN	of St Albans
AHRB	researchers	ALCM	killer; missile; weapon
AHS	in the year of human salvation	ALD	alderman; illness
		ALF	Alfred; Animal Liberation Front; liberationists
AHV	at this word		
AI	Amnesty International; artificial insemination; artificial intelligence; fertility treatment	ALG	algebra; algebraic; Algeria
		ALI	Alice; Alicia; Alison; Alisson; Allison
		ALP	party
A1	capital; élite; excellent; fine; first-class; first-rate; high-class; ideal; perfect; road; super; superb; wonderful	ALPA	pilots
		ALS	condition; illness
		ALT	alternate; altitude; alto
		ALU	arithmetic logic unit; unit
AIA	actuary		
AIB	banker(s)	AM	Albert Medal; amateur; America; American; americium; amplitude modulation; ante meridiem; associate member; before noon; degree; early; Hail Mary; in the morning; in the year of the world; Master of Arts; member; morning; parliamentarian; scholar
AID	artificial insemination; fertility treatment; fertilization		
AIDS	condition; illness; infection; syndrome		
AIFA	financial advisers		
AIH	artificial insemination; fertility treatment; fertilization		
AIM	Alternative Investment Market	AMA	doctors
		AMCS	system
A1M	road	AMDG	to the greater glory of God
AK	Alaska; knight; Knight of Australia		
		AMER	America; American
AKA	also called; also known as; also named	AMEX	American Express®; American Stock Exchange; credit card; plastic providers; trust
AKST	Alaska Standard Time; Alaska Time		
		AMP	ampere; amplifier

abbreviation ⇨ full form

AMR	automatic message routeing	AONB	area of outstanding natural beauty
AMRAAM	missile; weapon	AOR	adult-oriented rock; album-oriented rock; aorist; music
AMSL	above mean sea level		
AMT	amount; quantity	AP	additional premium; Air Police; American plan; anti-personnel; apothecary; apparent; apparently; Associated Press; author's proof; before a meal; Herbert; police; press
AMU	atomic mass unit; unit		
AN	actinon; Anglo-Norman; Angola; anonymous; ante; before; in the year		
ANAL	analogous; analogy; analysis; analytic; analytical		
ANAT	anatomic; anatomy	APA	publishers
ANC	African National Congress; ancient; anciently	APB	all-points bulletin
		APC	armoured personnel carrier; automatic public convenience; drug; toilet
AND	Andorra; circuit		
ANFO	explosive	APEX	advance purchase excursion; staff association; ticket
ANG	in English		
ANL	Anti-Nazi League		
ANME	limited liability	APH	Herbert
ANON	anonymous; name unknown	APL	language; programming language
		APO	apogee
ANS	answer; autonomic nervous system; solution; system	APOC	Apocalypse; apocrypha; apocryphal
ANSI	American Standards Association	APP	apparent; apparently; appendix; applied; apprentice; approved; approximate
ANTIQ	antiquarian; antiques; antiquities		
ANU	university	APPROX	about; approximate; approximately; around
AO	Army Order; Officer of (the Order of) Australia	APR	annual percentage rate; annualized percentage rate; April; interest; month; rate; weeks
AOB	any other business		
AOC	Air Officer Commanding; appellation contrôlée; appellation d'origine contrôlée; designation of wines	APT	advanced passenger train; apartment; train
		AQ	achievement quotient; aqueous; liquid; solution; water
AOK	all items satisfactory		
AOL	America Online; Internet service provider		

115

AR	airman recruit; annual return; Arab; Arabia; Arabian; Arabic; Aramaic; argon; Arkansas; army regulation; aspect ratio; autonomous region; gas	ART	article; artificial; artillery
		ARTY	artillery
		AS	air speed; air staff; all sections; Anglo-Saxon; antisubmarine; arsenic; assistant secretary; examination; in the year of salvation; metalloid
ARA	academician; Aircraft Research Association; artist; researchers; rowers	ASA	Advertising Standards Authority; American Standards Association; swimmers
ARAB	Arabia; Arabian; Arabic		
ARB	arbitrageur; Architects Registration Board	ASAP	as soon as possible
ARC	Aeronautical Research Council; AIDS-related complex	ASB	Accounting Standards Board
		ASBM	missile; weapon
ARCCOS	arc cosine	ASH	Action on Smoking and Health
ARCH	archaic; archaism; archery; archipelago; architect; architectural; architecture	ASL	American Sign Language; language
		ASLEF	railwaymen
ARCHD	archdeacon; archduke; clergyman; clergywoman	ASM	assistant stage manager; killer; missile; weapon
ARCHIT	architect; architectural; architecture	ASR	air-sea rescue; answer, send and receive; automatic send and receive; detector
ARCSIN	arc sine		
ARCTAN	arc tangent		
ARD	acute respiratory disease; condition; illness	ASS; ASSOC	associate; associated; association
ARG	arginine	ASST	assistant
ARITH	arithmetic; arithmetical	AST	advanced skills teacher; advanced supersonic transport; Alaska Standard Time; Alaska Time; Atlantic Standard Time; Atlantic Time; automatic station tuning; teacher
ARIZ	Arizona		
ARK	Arkansas		
ARLA	letting agents		
ARM	Armenian; Armoric		
ARP	air-raid precautions		
ARR	arranged; arranged by; arranger; arrival; arrived; arrives; arriving; in the year of the King's reign; in the year of the Queen's reign	ASTR; ASTRON	astronomer, astronomical, astronomy
		ASW	antisubmarine warfare
ARSA	artist		

AT	administrative trainee; alternative technology; anti-tank; appropriate technology; astatine; Atlantic Standard Time; Atlantic Time	AUFL	edition
		AUG	augmentative; August; month; weeks
		AUGM	augmentative; enlarged
ATA	Air Transport Association; Air Transport Auxiliary; auxiliaries	AUI	Attachment Unit Interface
		AUS	Australia
		AUST; AUSTR	Australia; Australian
ATC	Air Training Corps; air-traffic control; automatic train control; trainers	AUT	teachers
		AV	alternative vote; April; audiovisual; authorized version; avenue; average; Bible; lawyer; lived; lived so many years; road; street; way
ATD	actual time of departure		
ATL	teachers		
ATM	atmosphere; atmospheric; automatic teller machine; missile; weapon	AVA	audiovisual aid(s)
		AVC	additional voluntary contribution; automatic volume control
ATNO	atomic number		
ATNUMB	atomic number	AVE	avenue; average; road; street; way
ATP	advanced turboprop; automatic train protection; engine	AVI	automatic vehicle identification
ATS	army; at the suit of; auxiliaries; serum; service; soldiers	AVM	air vice-marshal; automatic vending machine
ATT	attorney	AVR	army; Army Volunteer Reserve
ATTN	for the attention of		
ATTRIB	attributed; attributive; attributively	AWACS	system
		AWE	Atomic Weapons Establishment
ATTY	attorney		
ATV	all-terrain vehicle; broadcasters	AWOL	absent; deserted; missing; unaccounted for
ATWT	atomic weight	AWU	atomic weight unit; unit
AU	African Union; Ångström unit; astronomical unit(s); gold; Organization of African Unity; unionists; unit	AX	axiom
		AZ	Arizona; Azed; Azerbaijan; street map
		AZT	azidothymidine; drug
AUC	from the founding of the city; in the year from the building of the city		

B	bachelor; baron; barrel(s); baryon number; bass; bedbug; bee; Belgium; billion; bishop; black; blood group; bomber; book; born; boron; bowled; boy; bravo; breadth; Britain; British; dismissed; key; low; magnetic flux density; man; metalloid; note; piece; road; second; second letter; secondary; second-class; second-rate; soft; three hundred; three thousand; vitamin; 300; 3,000	BARTS	hospital; school
		BAS	agriculturist; British Antarctic Survey
		BASF	company; multinational; multinational chemical company
		BASW	social workers
		BAT	Bartholomew; battalion; battery
		BATT	battalion; battery
		BAZ	Barry; Basil
BA	academy; airline; bachelor; Bachelor of Arts; barium; booksellers; British Academy; degree; graduate; scholar	BB	bed and breakfast; books; Boys' Brigade; Brigitte Bardot; very black; very soft
		BBA	bankers
		BBC	Auntie; broadcasters; network
BAA	British Airports Authority	BBL	barrels
BAB	Barbara	BBQ	barbecue
BAC	airline; baccalaureate; degree; system	BBS	bulletin board system; forum; system
BACH	bachelor	BC	ancient times; battery commander; before Christ; board of control; British Columbia; British Council
BACS	payment system; system of transferring money		
BAE	British Aerospace		
BAF	athletes	BCC	blind carbon copy
BAGR; BAGRIC	agriculturist	BCD	binary coded decimal
		BCE	before the Common Era
BAI	engineer	BCF	cyclists; fire extinguisher
BAL	balance; blood alcohol level	BCG	vaccination; vaccine
		BCH	surgeon
BALPA	pilots	BCL	lawyer
BANDB	bed and breakfast	BCOM	degree
BAOR	army	BCS	British Computer Society; society
BAP; BAPT	Baptist; baptized		
BAR	baritone; barrister; Baruch	BD	Bangladesh; bank draft; bills discounted; board; bond; bound; degree; theologian
BARCH	architect		
BART	baronet		

BDA	British Deaf Association; dentists	BHS	store
		BI	AC/DC; bisexual; bismuth
BDE	brigade		
BDI	Federation of German Industries	BIB	Bible
		BIBA	brokers
BDR	bombardier	BIBL	biblical; bibliographical; bibliography
BDS	Barbados; dentist		
BE	beryllium; bill of exchange; Board of Education; engineer	BIDS	Internet service; Internet system
		BIFU	bankers
BEA	airline; Beatrice; Beatrix	BIH	Bosnia and Herzegovina
BECTU	broadcasters	BIO	biography
BEDS	Bedfordshire	BIOL	biology
BEE	Beatrice; Beatrix	BIOS	basic input-output system; computer system; operating system
BEF	before; British Expeditionary Force; force		
BEL	Annabel; Annabella; Annabelle; Arabella; Isabel; Isabella; Isbel; Ishbel; Isobel	BIS	bank; Bank for International Settlements
		BIT	binary digit
		BIZ	business
BELG	Belgian; Belgium	BJP	Hindu nationalists; nationalists; party
BEM	British Empire Medal		
BEN	Benjamin	BK	bank; berkelium; book
BENG	engineer	BKG	banking
BERKS	Berkshire	BKS	barracks; books
BES	Business Expansion Scheme	BL	bale; barrel; bill of lading; British Legion; British Library; car manufacturers; company; lawyer; library
BESS	scientist		
BET	between; Elizabeth		
BEV	billion electronvolts		
BEX	Rebecca	BLDG	building
BF	bloody fool; bold face; brought forward; Burkina Faso; fool; type	BLT	sandwich filling
		BLVD	boulevard; road; street; way
BFBS	broadcasters	BM	airline; British Museum; doctor; museum
BFPO	military postal service		
BG	Bulgaria	BMA	doctors
BH	Belize; bohrium; British Honduras	BMG	record company; record producer
		BMI	airline; body mass index
BHC	insecticide; killer	BMUS	musician
BHP	brake horsepower		

BMW	automobile; Bavarian Motor Works; car; car manufacturers	BRAZ	Brazil; Brazilian
		BRIG	brigadier
BN	baron; battalion; billion	BRIT	Britain; Britannia; British; Briton
BNP	fascists; nationalists; party	BRN	Bahrain
BO	body odour; box office; branch office; buyer's option; hum; odour; smell	BRO	blood relative; brother; fellow; relation; relative; sibling
		BROS	brothers
BOAC	airline	BRS	British Road Services
BOB	Robert	BRU	Brunei
BOD	body; person	BS	The Bahamas; balance sheet; bill of sale; British Standard(s); building society; nonsense; scientist; society; surgeon
BOGOF	buy one get one free		
BOHO	bohemian		
BOL	Bolivia		
BOR	borough; neighbour	BSA	Business Software Alliance
BOT	botanical; botany; bottle; robot	BSC	Bachelor of Science; Building Societies Commission; degree; graduate; scientist
BOUL	boulevard		
BP	before 1950; before present; bills payable; birthplace; bishop; blood pressure; boiling point; clergyman; clergywoman; company; oil company		
		BSE	illness; infection
		BSM	British School of Motoring; school
		BST	British Summer Time; drug; summertime
BPHARM	pharmacist	BT	baronet; insecticide; killer; telephone company
BPHIL	philosopher		
BPI	bits per inch; bytes per inch		
		BTCV	conservationists; preservationists
BPL	birthplace		
BPM	beats per minute; rate	BTU	Board of Trade unit; unit
BPS	bits per second; psychologists; rate	BTW	by the way
		BU	bushel(s)
BQ	becquerel(s); unit	BUCKS	Buckinghamshire
BR	bank rate; bedroom; bills receivable; branch; Brazil; bridge; Britain; British; British Rail; bromine; bronze; brother; brown; lines; railway; rate	BUD	companion
		BULG	Bulgaria; Bulgarian
		BUNAC	club
		BUPA	insurers; medical insurers
BRA	brassière; support; supporter; underwear	BUS	business

BV	Blessed Virgin; company; farewell; firm; limited company	BY	Belarus
		BYE	farewell
		BYO	bring your own
BVM	Blessed Virgin Mary	BYOB	bring your own beer; bring your own booze; bring your own bottle
BW	black and white		
BWR	boiling-water reactor		
BWV	Bach's works; catalogue of Bach's works; works by Bach	BZ	Belize

C

C	about; approximately; around; calorie; canine; capacitance; cape; caput; carat; carbon; care of; cargo transport; Catholic; caught; caught by; Celsius; cent; centigrade; centimes; century; Chambers; chapter; Charlie; circa; clef; cloudy; clubs; cocaine; cold; college; coloured; colt; command paper; common time; compliance; congestion; conservative; constant; contralto; copyright; corps; coulomb; Cuba; cubic; dismissed; electrical capacitance; great number; heaps; hundred; hundred dollars; hundred thousand; key; kilocalorie(s); large number; load(s); lot(s); many; note; party; see; speed of light; tap; third-rate; ton; unit; vitamin; 100; $100
CA	about; accountant; approximately; army; around; calcium; California; capital account; cases; Central America; Chartered Accountant; chief accountant; Church Army; circa; consular agent; Consumers' Association; county alderman; credit account; current account; watchdog
CAA	Civil Aviation Authority
CAB	car; Citizens' Advice Bureau

CABG	coronary artery bypass graft
CACM	common market; community; market
CAD	computer-aided design; computer-aided drafting; disc; record
CAE	computer-aided engineering
CAERNS	Caernarvonshire
CAF	cost and freight
CAI	computer-aided instruction
CAL	calendar; calibre; California; calorie; computer-aided learning; computer-assisted learning; kilocalorie(s)
CALIF	California
CAM	Cameroon; computer-aided manufacture; computer-aided manufacturing
CAMB	Cambridge; Cambridgeshire
CAMBS	Cambridgeshire
CAMRA	Campaign for Real Ale
CAN	Canada; Canadian; canal; Canberra; canon; canto; canton
CANC	cancellation; cancelled
CAND	Campaign Against Nuclear Dumping
CANDB	caught and bowled; caught and bowled by; dismissed
CANDF	cost and freight
CANDG	City and Guilds Institute
CANT	Canterbury; canticles
CANTAB	of Cambridge
CANTUAR	Canterbury

CAP	capacity; capital; capital letter; capitalize; chapter; Common Agricultural Policy; computer-aided production; EU policy; let her/him take	CBIS	computer-based information system; system
		CBS	network
CAPEX	capital expenditure	CBSO	orchestra
CAPS	capital letters; capitals; upper case	CBT	computer-based training
		CC	Cape Colony; Cape Coloured; carbon copies; carbon copy; chapters; closed-circuit; club; Competition Commission; confined to camp; county council; county councillor; cricket club; croquet club; cubic centimetre(s); 200
CAPT	captain		
CAR	compound annual rate; compounded annual rate; rate		
CARD	Campaign Against Racial Discrimination; cardinal		
CARDS	Cardiganshire		
CARIBB	Caribbean	CCC	club; county cricket club; cricket club; 300
CARICOM	Caribbean Community; common market; community; market	CCD	charge-coupled device
		CCF	Central Control Function; chronic heart failure; Combined Cadet Force
CAT	boat; catalogue; catalytic converter; catamaran; catechism; caterpillar; college; computer-aided training; computer-assisted training; scan; scanner; tractor		
		CCL	250
		CCMI	companion; manager
		CCR	camera cassette recorder; critical compression ratio; recorder
CATH	cathedral; cathode; Catholic	CCT	compulsory competitive tendering
CAV	the court wishes to be advised	CCTV	closed-circuit television; television
CB	centre of buoyancy; Citizens' Band; columbium; companion; Companion of the Bath; confined to barracks; confinement; county borough; radio	CCU	coronary care unit; hospital department; unit
		CD	cadmium; candela; carried down; cash discount; civil defence; coefficient of drag; command paper; compact disc; contagious disease(s); controlled drug; defence; diplomat(s); diplomatic corps; disc; large number; many; record; unit; 400
CBC	broadcasters		
CBD	cash before delivery		
CBE	commander		
CBI	Confederation of British Industry		
		CDI	disc

C

CDN	Canada; Canadian	CFC	gas
CDR	commander; disc	CFD	computational fluid dynamics
CDRE	commodore		
CDROM; CDRW	disc	CFE	army; college
		CFG	cubic feet of gas
CDSO	companion	CFI	cost, freight, insurance
CDT	craft, design, technology	CFO	financial officer; fire officer
CDV	Civil Defence Volunteer(s); virus; volunteers	CFP	banks; Common Fisheries Policy; French Pacific Banks; French Pacific Colonies
CE	Anglican; cerium; chancellor; chemical engineer; chief engineer; church; Church of England; civil engineer; common entrance; Common Era; Council of Europe; engineer; safety mark; treasurer	CFR	commercial fast reactor
		CFS	chronic fatigue syndrome; illness; syndrome
		CFT	cubic feet; cubic foot
		CG	captain of the guard; captain-general; centigram(s); centigramme(s); centre of gravity; coastguard; Coldstream Guards; commanding general; consul general; Croix de Guerre; guards; weight
CEL	celebrated; film		
CELT	Celtic		
CEN	central; century		
CENG	chartered engineer; engineer		
CENT	centigrade; central; century; hundred		
CEO	executive officer	CGA	colour graphics adapter
CERN	researchers	CGE	carriage
CERT	certificate; certificated; certified; certify	CGEFWD	carriage-forward
		CGEPD	carriage-paid
CERTED	certificate	CGI	City and Guilds Institute
CERTIF	certificate; certificated; certified; certify	CGO	Congo: Democratic Republic of
CET	Central European Time	CGS	centimetre-gram-second; Chief of General Staff
CF	californium; carried forward; centre-forward; compare; cost and freight; forces' chaplain	CGT	capital gains tax; tax; trade union
CFA	African Financial Community; community; French African Colonies		
CFANDI	cost, freight and insurance		

CH	boilers, radiators, *etc*; central heating; centre-half; chain; champion; chaplain; chapter; chart; check; chestnut; chief; child; children; China; Chinese; choir; Christ; Chronicles; church; clearing house; clubhouse; companion; Companion of Honour; court house; customs house; heating system; honourable companion; surgeon; Switzerland	CI	Channel Islands; Côte d'Ivoire; curie; Ivory Coast; 101
		CIA	business; company; firm; intelligence; intelligence service; spies; spooks
		CIB	bankers; investigators; police
		CIC	commander-in-chief; top brass
		CID	detectives; investigators; police
CHAE	Charles	CIE	business; companion; company; firm; Transport Organization of Ireland
CHAMB	chamberlain		
CHANC	chancellor; chancery	CIF	cost, insurance, freight
CHAP	chaplain; chapter; clergyman; clergywoman	CIGS	Chief of the Imperial General Staff
CHAPS	payment system; system; system of transferring money	CII	insurers
		CIM	computer input on microfilm; computer integrated manufacture
CHB	surgeon	CINC	commander-in-chief; general; top brass
CHD	condition; coronary heart disease; illness		
CHE	chemical engineer; engineer	CIO	Congress of Industrial Organizations
CHEM	chemical; chemistry	CIOJ	journalists
CHES	Cheshire	CIP	cataloguing in publication
CHG	charge		
CHIN	China; Chinese	CIPA	patent agents
CHJ	Chief Justice; judge; justice	CIR; CIRC	about; approximately; around
CHM	chairman; checkmate; degree; Master of Surgery; surgeon	CIS	cataloguing in source; Cecilia; Cecily; Cicely; Commonwealth of Independent States
CHMN	chairman	CIT	citation; citizen
CHP	combined heat and power	CIV	civil; civilian
CHR	Christ; Christian	CJ	civil justice; judge
CHRON	chronicle; Chronicles; chronological; chronology	CJD	condition; illness; infection

CL	centilitre(s); chlorine; class; gas; hundred and fifty; Sri Lanka; 150
CLA	acid
CLASS	classical; classification
CLEAR	Campaign for Lead-free Air
CLIT; CLITT	companion; Companion of Literature
CLLR	councillor
CLO	close; road; street; way
CLP	party
CLR	computer language recorder
CLT	computer language translator
CLX	160
CM	by reason of death; centimetre(s); command paper; Congregation of the Mission; corresponding member; curium; degree; Master of Surgery; metric carat; surgeon; 900
CMD	command paper
CMDR	commander
CMG	companion
CMI	computer-managed instruction
CML	computer-managed learning
CMND	command paper
CMS	Church Mission Society; society
CMV	virus
CN	Canadian National; credit note
CNAG	Gaelic developer
CNAR	compound net annual rate; rate

CND	anti-nuclear group; Campaign for Nuclear Disarmament
CNN	broadcasters; certified nursery nurse; nurse
CNS	central nervous system; system
CO	business; carbon monoxide; care of; cobalt; Colombia; Colorado; combined operations; commanding officer; Commonwealth Office; company; conscientious objector; county; Crown Office; firm; gas; leader
COAD	coadjutor
COBRA	national emergency action committee
COD	cash on delivery; codex; collect on delivery
COE	Council of Europe
COED	computer-operated electronic display
COFA	certificate
COFC	chamber of commerce
COFE	Anglican; church; Church of England; Council of Europe
COFI	church; Church of Ireland
COFS	Chief of Staff; church; Church of Scotland
COG	cognate
COI	Central Office of Information
COL	colonel; Colorado; Colossians; colour; column; computer-orientated language; language; programming language
COLA	cost-of-living adjustment

COLL	colleague; collective; collector; college; colloquial
COLLAT	collateral; collaterally
COLLOQ	colloquial; colloquially
COLO	Colorado
COLOG	cologarithm
COLOSS	Colossians
COM	comedy; commander; commerce; commissioner; committee; commodore; common; commonwealth; commune; communist; computer output on microfilm
COMDR	commander
COMDT	commandant
COMINT	communications intelligence
COMM	commander; commentary; communication
COMMN	commission
COMP	accompanist; comparative; compare; compiler; composer; compound; compounded; comprehensive; comprising
COMPAR	comparative; comparison
COMR	commissioner
CON	against; conclusion; confidence; conformist; conservation; conservative; Constance; consul; convict; do; party; politician; prisoner; trick
CONC	concentrated; concentration
CONG	congregation; congregational; congress; congressional; gallon
CONJ	conjunction; conjunctive
CONN	connected; Connecticut; connection
CONS	consecrated; conservative; consigned; consignment; consolidated; consonant; constable; constitution; constitutional; construction; consulting
CONST	constant; constitution
CONSTR	construction
CONT; CONTD	continued
CONTR	contracted; contraction
COP	certificate; Certificate of Proficiency; pass; police officer
COPD	condition; emphysema; illness
COR	Corinthians; corner; cornet; coroner
CORE	Congress of Racial Equality
CORGI	gas installers
CORN	Cornish; Cornwall
COROL	corollary
CORP	corporal; corporation
CORR	correspond; corrupted; corruption
CORRES	corresponding
COS	Chief of Staff; cosine; function; function of an angle
COSEC	cosecant; function; function of an angle
COSECH	function; function of an angle; hyperbolic cosecant
COSH	function; function of an angle; hyperbolic cosine
COT	cotangent; function; function of an angle

COTH	function; function of an angle; hyperbolic cotangent	CPS	characters per second; Crown Prosecution Service; cycles per second; prosecutors; rate
COV	covariance; crossover value	CPU	central processing unit; unit
COVERS	coversed sine; function	CPVE	certificate
COX	coxswain	CQ	transmitted by an amateur operator
COY	company		
COZ	cousin	CR	carriage return; chromium; community; Costa Rica; councillor; credit; creditor; crown; King Charles
CP	candle-power; chemically pure; command post; Common Prayer; Communist Party; compare; compiler; Congregation of the Passion; party		
		CRC	camera-ready copy
		CRES	crescent; road; street; way
CPA	accountant	CRESC	becoming louder; crescendo
CPAG	Child Poverty Action Group	CRIMCON	criminal conversation
CPD	compound	CRIT	critical; criticism
CPG	Coronary Prevention Group	CRO	cathode-ray oscilloscope; Criminal Records Office
CPGB	party	CRT	cathode-ray tube; composite rate tax; tax
CPI	characters per inch; consumer price index	CS	caesium; chartered surveyor; Christian Science; civil service; Clerk to the Signet; court; Court of Session; cycles per second; gas; hertz; rate; surveyor
CPL	corporal; non-commissioned officer		
CPM	characters per minute; computer system; operating system; rate; system		
		CSA	Child Support Agency; Confederate States of America
CPO	Chief Petty Officer; crime prevention officer; petty officer	CSC	Civil Service Commission
CPP	current purchasing power	CSE	certificate; Combined Services Entertainment; entertainers; examination; forces' entertainers; School Certificate
CPR	railway; resuscitation		
CPRE	conservationists; preservationists		
CPRS	Central Policy Review Staff; government think-tank		
		CSF	cerebrospinal fluid
		CSM	Committee on Safety of Medicines

CSO	community-service order	CVA	accident; cerebrovascular accident; haemorrhage
CSP	physiotherapists	CVT	continuous variable transmission
CST	Central Standard Time; craniosacral therapy; therapy	CW	chemical warfare
CSV	community-service volunteer; volunteer	CWC	chemical weapons convention
CT	carat; caught; caught by; cent; Central Time; Connecticut; court; scan; scanner; weight	CWD	chronic wasting disease; condition; illness
CTC	club; cyclists; Cyclists' Touring Club	CWO	cash with order
		CWT	hundredweight(s); weight
CTOL	aircraft; airplane	CWU	Communication Workers Union
CTS	syndrome	CX	110
CTT	capital transfer tax; tax	CY	Cyprus; Cyrus
CU	copper; cubic	CYM	Cymric; Welsh
CUB	cubic	CZ	Czech Republic
CUMB	Cumbria		
CUP	press; publishers		
CUR	current; this month		
CURT	current; this month		
CV	chevaux; course of life; Cross of Valour; cultivar; cultivated variety; curriculum vitae; education and achievement details; progress of life; résumé; 105		

D	catalogue of Schubert's works; coin; copper; date; daughter; day; dead; deceased; dee; degree; delete; delta; Democrat; Democratic; density; depart; departed; department; departs; depth; deserted; deuterium; Deutsch; diameter; diamonds; did; died; dimension; dinar; director; displacement; dollar; down; duke; Dutch; electric flux; five hundred; flux; fourth-rate; Germany; God; great number; had; heaps; key; large number; late; load(s); lord; lot(s); many; note; old pence; old penny; party; pence; penny; Schubert's works; time; vitamin; works by Schubert; would; 500; 500,000	DAP	distributed array processor
		DAR	Daughters of the American Revolution
		DAT	case; dative
		DATEC	data and telecommunications
		DAU	daughter
		DB	decibel(s); dubnium
		DBE	dame
		DBL	double
		DBMS	system
		DBS	satellite
		DC	chiropractor; current; da capo; detective; direct current; district; district commissioner; District of Columbia; doctor; police officer; return to the beginning; to the beginning; Washington; 600
DA	blood relative; dad; digital-to-analogue; dinar; diploma; district attorney; father; hairstyle; lawyer; prosecutor; relation; relative	DCB	dame
		DCC	digital compact cassette
		DCF	discounted cash flow
		DCH	surgeon
		DCI	detective
		DCL	lawyer
		DCM	district court martial
DAB	digital audio broadcasting	DCMG	dame
DAD	blood relative; father; relation; relative	DCMS	department
		DCVO	dame
DAI	Dafydd; David; Welshman	DD	days after date; day's date; designated driver; direct debit; divine; doctor; Doctor of Divinity; donated; gave as a gift; gave to God; theologian
DAL	decalitre(s)		
DALY	disability-adjusted life year		
DAM	decametre(s)		
DAN	Daniel; Danish	DDAY	invasion day
DANDC	obstetric treatment; scrape	DDD	gave and dedicated as a gift; gives, devotes and dedicates
DANDD	drunk and disorderly		

DDE	computer system; dynamic data exchange; system	DET	detective
		DETR	department
		DEUT	Deuteronomy
DDR	East Germany; German Democratic Republic	DEW	distant early warning
		DEX	drug; stimulant
DDS	dentist; digital data storage; doctor	DF	defender of the faith; direction finder
DDT	fly-killer; insecticide; killer	DFES; DFID	department
DE	Delaware; department	DFT	defendant; department; draft
DEA	department; Drug Enforcement Administration	DG	by the grace of God; decigram(s); decigramme(s); director-general; weight
DEB	beginner; Deborah; Debra; debutante; girl; one coming out	DH	department; ie; Lawrence; that is
DEC	deceased; December; declaration; declension; departed; died; Disasters Emergency Committee; last month; month; present month; weeks	DHSS	department
		DI	artificial insemination; condition; Deanna; Deanne; Defence Intelligence; detective; detective inspector; diabetes; Dian; Diana; Diane; Dianne; donor insemination; fertility treatment; fertilization; girl; illness; police officer; princess; 501
DECL	declension		
DED	doctor		
DEE	damn		
DEF	defendant; definition		
DEFRA	department		
DEG	degree(s)		
DEL	Delaware; delegate; Derek; Derrick; Deryck; drew; he/she drew	DIA	diameter
		DIAL	dialect
		DIAM	diameter
DEM	Democrat; Democratic; party	DIANE	network
		DIC	diploma
DEN	Denis; Dennis; Denys	DICT	dictation; dictator; dictionary
DENG	doctor; engineer		
DENI	department	DIE	Deanna; Deanne; Dian; Diana; Diane; Dianne
DENT	dental; dentist; dentistry		
DEP	depart; department; departs; departure; deposed; deposit; deputy	DIF	data interchange format
		DIFF	difference; different
		DIG	Disablement Income Group
DEPT	department; deputy		
DER; DERIV	derivation; derivative; derived	DIH	diploma

DIL	dilute	DMA	direct memory access
DIM	becoming quieter; dimension; diminuendo; diminutive	DMARK	Deutschmark
		DMD	illness
DIMIN	becoming quieter; diminuendo; diminutive	DMO	district medical officer; doctor
		DMS	footwear; system
DIMM	dual in-line memory module	DMSO	medical solvent; solvent
DING	doctor; engineer	DMUS	doctor; musician
DIP; DIPED; DIPSW; DIPTECH	diploma	DMZ	demilitarized zone
		DN	down
		DNA	acid; deoxyribonucleic acid; means of identification
DIR	director		
DIS	discontinued; disrespect; treat with contempt	DNB	dictionary
DISC	discount; discoverer	DNR	dinar; do not resuscitate
DISS	discourse; thesis; treatise	DNS	domain name system; system
DIST	distance; distilled; distinguish; district	DO	ditto; dominee; Dorothea; Dorothy; likewise; note
DIV	divide; dividend; divine; division; divorce; divorced; share	DOA	date of availability; dead on arrival
DIY	do-it-yourself; homework; housework	DOB	date of birth; Robert
DJ	deejay; disc jockey; jacket; Jock; record player; tuxedo	DOC	appellation contrôlée; appellation d'origine contrôlée; designation of wines; district officer commanding; doctor; file format
DK	dark; deck; Denmark; dock		
DL	decilitre(s); demand loan; Deputy Lieutenant; 550	DOCG	designation of wines
DLA	disability living allowance	DOD; DOE	department
DLIT; DLITT	doctor	DOH	department; note
DLL	dynamic link library; library	DOL	dolce; dollar; gently; sweetly
DLO	dead-letter office	DOLS	dollars
DLP	party	DOM	belonging to the Lord; brother; dirty old man; domestic; Dominical; Dominican; Dominican Republic; dominion; friar; God; lord; to God, the best, the greatest
DLR	dealer		
DLVY	delivery		
DM	condition; decimetre(s); Deutschmark; diabetes; illness; mark		

DOMS	diploma	DSA	Driving Standards Agency
DON	Donald		
DOR	Doric	DSC	doctor
DORA	Defence of the Realm Act	DSL	digital subscriber line; Internet connection
DORS	Dorset		
DOS	computer system; disk operating system; operating system; system	DSP	died without issue
		DSS	department; director
		DST	daylight saving time; wouldst
DOT	Dorothea; Dorothy		
DOTS	directly observed therapy, short-course; therapy; tuberculosis treatment	DT	data transmission; delirium tremens; jitters; shakes
DOZ	dozen; twelve; 12	DTH; DTHEOL	doctor; theologian
DP	data processing; displaced person	DTI; DTLR	department
DPA	Data Protection Authority; Discharged Prisoners' Aid; protectionists	DTP	desktop publishing
		DTS	delirium tremens; jitters; shakes
		DU	depleted uranium; Dutch
DPH	diploma; doctor; philosopher	DUD	Dudley
		DUI	driving under the influence
DPHIL	doctor; philosopher		
DPI	dots per inch	DUNELM	of Durham
DPM	diploma	DUP	duplicate; party; unionists
DPP	director		
DPT	department; dioptre; vaccination; vaccine	DUR	Durham
		DV	drive; God willing; 505
DR	debtor; doctor; drachma; dram; drawer; drive; driver; drummer; dry riser; Grace; healer; road; street; way	DVD	disc; record
		DVT	deep-vein thrombosis
		DWP	department
		DWT	dead-weight tonnage
DRAM	memory; store	DX	510
DRV	dietary reference values	DY	Benin; Dahomey; dysprosium
DS	condition; dal segno; detective; detective sergeant; doctor; document signed; illness; police officer; return to the sign; surgeon; to the sign		
		DYN	dynamo; dynamometer; dyne
		DZ	Algeria; dozen; twelve; 12

E	base; cardinal point; constant; direction; drug; earl; earth; east; eastern; eccentricity; echo; ecstasy; Edward; electric field strength; electromotive force; electron; electronic; electronic charge; Elizabeth; energy; English; estimate; European; force; key; layer; mail; note; opponent; orient; oriental; part of London; partner; player; point; quarter; Spain; stimulant; tablet; two hundred and fifty; two hundred and fifty thousand; vitamin; way; 250; 250,000	EC	church; city; community; East Caribbean; east central; Ecuador; Established Church; European Commission; European Community; executive committee; locality; market; part of London
		ECB	bank; cricket board; England and Wales Cricket Board
		ECCL; ECCLES	Ecclesiastes; ecclesiastical
		ECCLUS	Ecclesiasticus
		ECE	Economic Commission for Europe
		ECG	electrocardiogram; electrocardiograph; hospital department; medical specialism
EA	each; East Africa; East Anglia; environment agency; environmentalists; per	ECM	electronic countermeasures
EAK	Kenya	ECO	green; orchestra
EAON	except as otherwise noted	ECOL	ecological; ecology
EAP	English for academic purposes	ECOLI	bacteria; bacterium
EAT	Tanzania	ECON	economic; economical; economics; economy
EAU	Uganda	ECOWAS	common market; community
EB	Epstein-Barr; illness; virus	ECS	satellite
EBD	emotional and behavioural difficulties; emotional and behavioural disorder	ECSC	community
		ECT	electroconvulsive therapy; therapy
EBOR	York; of York	ECUK	Engineering Council UK
EBRD	bank	ECUSA	church
EBU	broadcasters	ED	boss; chief; Edgar; edited; edition; editor; Edmund; educated; education; Edward; Edwin; journalist; leader; press employee; Spenser
EBV	Epstein-Barr virus; virus		
		EDC	community; ethylene dichloride

EDD	doctor	EGM	meeting
EDI	electronic data interchange	EGU	English Golf Union; golfers
EDIN	Edinburgh	EHF	extremely high frequency
EDIT	edited; edition; editor	EHO	environmental health officer; environmentalist
EDO	memory		
EDORAM	memory; store	EI	East Indian; East Indies
EDP	electronic data processing	EIA	environmental impact assessment
EDS	English Dialect Society; society	EIB	bank
EDTA	acid; chelating agent	EIS	Educational Institute of Scotland; Enterprise Investment Scheme
EDY	Edith		
EE	early English; errors excepted	EJUSD	of the same
EEA	environmentalists	EKCO	electrical manufacturer
EEC	common market; community; market	EL	elevated railroad; railroad; railway
EED	electro-explosive device	ELEC; ELECT	electric; electricity
EEF	Engineering Employers' Federation	ELF	extra low frequency; extremely low frequency
EEG	electroencephalogram; electroencephalograph	ELIEN	of Ely
		ELINT	electronic intelligence
EEN	even	ELT	English language teaching
EEPROM	memory; store	ELV	expendable launch vehicle
EER	ever		
EET	Eastern European Time	EM	Emma; Emily; them
EETS	Early English Text Society	EMA	engineers
EEZ	exclusive economic zone	EMF	electromagnetic field; electromagnetic force; electromotive force
EFA	acid; aircraft; essential fatty acid; fighter aircraft; warplane		
		EMG	electromyogram; electromyograph
EFL	English as a foreign language	EMI	company; electromagnetic interference; record company; record producer
EFT	electronic funds transfer		
EFTA	traders		
EG	as; equivalent grade; for example; for instance; illustration; say		
		EMM	Emma
		EMP	emperor; empire; empress
EGA	enhanced graphics adapter		

EMS	Emergency Medical Service; enhanced messaging service; expanded memory system; memory; system	EPA	acid; environmentalists
		EPG	bigwigs; Eminent Persons' Group
		EPH	Ephesians
EMU	Economic and Monetary Union; electric multiple unit; electromagnetic unit; European Monetary Union; unit	EPIPH	Epiphany
		EPIS	Episcopal; epistle
		EPNS	plate
		EPO	hormone
EN	Enrolled Nurse; nurse; opponents	EPOCH	End Physical Punishment of Children
ENA	Eugenia; Eugenie	EPOS	electronic point of sale
ENC; ENCL	enclosed; enclosure	EPP	party
ENCY; ENCYC; ENCYCL	book of knowledge; comprehensive	EPROM	memory; store
		EPS	earnings per share; file format
ENE	direction; east-north-east	EPT	environmental protection technology
ENG	electronic news gathering; engineer; engineering; England; English; engraver; engraving; Enrolled Nurse; nurse	EQ	equal; equation; equivalent
		ER	American soap; emergency room; erbium; king; King Edward; queen; Queen Elizabeth; soap; sovereign
ENO	English National Opera		
ENP	electronic number plate		
ENS	ensign	ERA	earned run average; Equal Rights Amendment
ENSA	entertainers; forces' entertainers	ERI	Edward, King and Emperor; king
ENT	entomology; hospital department; medical specialism	ERK	airman
		ERM	exchange rate mechanism
ENVEXT	envoy extraordinary	ERNIE	bond picker; computer; premium bond picker
EO	ex officio; executive officer	EROM	memory; store
EOC	Equal Opportunities Commission	ERV	endogenous retroviruses; retroviruses
EOD	every other day	ERW	enhanced radiation weapon
EOKA	Greek Cypriot unionists; unionists	ES	einsteinium; El Salvador; opponents
EOT	end of tape; end of transmission	ESA	environmentally sensitive area
EP	disc; electroplated; en passant; epistle; extreme pressure; record; single		

abbreviation ⇨ full form

E

ESB	electrical stimulation of the brain	ESU	electrostatic unit; English-Speaking Union; unit
ESC	Economic and Social Committee; escape; escudo; key	ET	alien; Eastern Time; Egypt; embryo transfer; employment trainee; employment training; ephemeris time; ethyl; extraterrestrial; film
ESCA	electron spectroscopy		
ESD	Esdras		
ESDA	electrostatic document analysis		
ESE	direction; east-south-east	ETA	estimated time of arrival; militants; separationists; separatists
ESL	English as a second language		
ESN	educationally subnormal; electronic serial number	ETAL	and elsewhere; and others
ESOL	English for speakers of other languages	ETB	Engineering and Technology Board; English Tourist Board; tourist board
ESOP	share ownership plan		
ESP	electro-selective pattern; electrostatic precipitator; English for specific purposes; epiphenomenon; especially; extrasensory perception; intuition; sixth sense	ETC	and so on; and the rest; English Tourism Council; et cetera; et ceteri
		ETH	Ethiopia
		ETI	inspectors
		ETSEQ; ETSQ	and what follows
		ETSU	Energy Technology Support Unit; unit
ESPEC	especially	ETY; ETYM; ETYMOL	etymological; etymology
ESPRIT	research programme		
ESQ; ESQR	esquire	EU	European Union; europium; Evangelical Union
ESR	electrical skin resistance; electron spin resonance		
ESRO	researchers	EUPH	euphemism; euphemistically
ESS	evolutionarily stable strategy	EUR	euro; Europe; European
ESSO	company; oil company	EV	Bible; electronvolt(s); English Version; Enigmatic Variations
EST	course; Eastern Standard Time; electric shock treatment; established; estate; estimated; Estonia; estuary; therapy		
		EVA	extravehicular activity; space walk; walk
		EVAN; EVANG	evangelical
ESTEC	researchers	EVGS	evenings
ESTH	Esther	EW	partners
		EWS	English, Welsh and Scottish Railway; railway

137

EX	dead; deceased; departed; died; examination; examined; example; except; excepted; exception; exchange; excursion; excursus; executed; executive; Exodus; export; express; extra; from; late; outside	EXLIB	ex libris; from the books of
		EXOD	Exodus
		EXOFF	by virtue of office; by virtue of position; ex officio
		EXON	Exeter; of Exeter
		EXOR	executor
EXC	excellency; excellent; except; exception; excursion; first-class; first-rate	EXP	experiment; experimental; expired; expiry; exponential; export; express
EXCH	exchange; exchequer	EXR	executor
EXCL	exclamation; excluding; exclusive	EXRX	executrix
		EXT	extension; exterior; external; externally; extinct; extra; extract
EXDIV	ex dividend; share purchase		
EXEC	board; board member; executive; executor	EXW	ex works
		EZ	Ezra
EXGR	as a favour; as an act of grace	EZEK	Ezekiel
		EZT	Enterprise Zone Trust

F	clef; coin; constant; copper; depth; Fahrenheit; farad; faraday; Faraday's constant; farthing; fathom(s); feet; fellow; female; feminine; fighter aircraft; filial generation; fine; fluorine; folio; following; foot; force; forte; forty; forty thousand; foxtrot; franc(s); France; frequency; furlong(s); gas; key; leaf; loud; noisy; note; page; strong; unit; warplane; woman; 40; 40,000	FBI	detectives; G-men; investigators; security agency
		FBR	fast-breeder reactor
		FC	church; club; football club; Forestry Commission; Free Church
		FCA; FCCA	accountant
		FCIB	banker
		FCMA	accountant
		FCS	chemist
		FD	defender of the faith
		FDA	First Division Association
		FDR	Free Democratic Republic; president; Roosevelt
FA	actuaries; Faculty of Actuaries; Fanny Adams; Florida; Football Association; footballers; note; nothing	FE	further education; iron; Smith
		FEB	February; month; weeks
		FEC	did; he/she did; he/she made; made
FAA	Fleet Air Arm	FED	agent; federal
FAB	excellent; fantastic; great; marvellous; terrific; wonderful	FEDS	detectives
		FEI	International Equestrian Federation
FACT	Federation Against Copyright Theft	FEM	feminine
FAH	note	FET	field-effect transistor
FAM	familiar; family	FF	did; fast forward; fellows; folios; following; form feed; fortissimo; franc (France); leaves; made; they did; they made it; pages
FAO	for the attention of		
FAQ	fair average quality; free alongside quay; frequently asked questions		
FAS	antiquarian; artist; foetal alcohol syndrome; free alongside ship; syndrome	FFF	fortississimo
		FIA	International Automobile Federation
FAST	Federation Against Software Theft	FIDDEF	defender of the faith
FAT	file allocation table	FIDE	World Chess Federation
FAX	copy; facsimile	FIDO	Fog Intensive Dispersal Operation

FIFA	International Football Federation	FOE	conservationists; environmentalists; preservationists
FIFO	first in, first out; redundancy order	FOL	folio; followed; following
FIG	figurative; figuratively; figure; International Gymnastics Federation	FOR	free on rail
		FOREST	smokers
		FOREX	foreign exchange
FILO	first in, last out; redundancy order	FP	fireplug; former pupil; fortepiano; Free Presbyterian; freezing point
FIN	Finland		
FINA	swimmers		
FINN	Finnish	FPA	Family Planning Association
FIS	dole; Family Income Supplement; grant; income support; International Ski Federation; skiers	FPS	feet per second; foot-pound-second; frames per second; rate
FISA	rowers	FR	father; fragment; France; francium; French; frequently; friar; Friday
FITA	archers		
FJI	Fiji; journalist	FRAT	brotherhood; fraternity; fraternize
FL	floor; Florida; florin; floruit; flourished; fluid; Liechtenstein		
		FRCA	anaesthetist
FLA	Florida	FRCP	doctor; physician
FLO	Flora; Florence	FRCS	surgeon
FLOR	Florida; florin; flourished	FRG	Germany
FLOZ	fluid ounce(s)	FRI	day; Friday
FLU	bug; illness; infection; influenza	FRPS	photographer
		FRSA	artist
FM	fathom; femtometre(s); fermium; field marshal; frequency modulation	FSA	antiquary; regulator
		FSB	security agency; small businesses
FMD	condition; illness; infection	FSH	full service history; hormone
FO	department; Faroe Islands; field officer; flying officer; folio; Foreign Office; full organ	FSS	Forensic Science Service
		FST	flatter squarer tube
		FT	daily; feet; Financial Times; foot; fort; full-time; journal; medium; newspaper; paper
FOB	free on board		
FOC	father of the chapel; free of charge	FTA	free trade agreement; Freight Transport Association

FTH; FTHM	fathom	FX	sound effects; special effects
FTSE	Financial Times Index; share index	FYA	first-year allowance
FUR	furlong	FYI	for your information
FUT	future	FZ	forzando; sforzando
FWD	forward; four-wheel drive; front-wheel drive	FZS	zoologist

G	acceleration due to gravity; classification; clef; conductance; constant; constant of gravitation; film classification; force; four hundred; four hundred thousand; Gabon; gallon(s); gauss; gee; general intelligence; George; German; girl; golf; good; gourde; government; Gräfenberg; gram(s); gramme(s); grand; gravity; group of; key; man; note; string; suit; thou; thousand; weight; 400; 1,000; £1,000; $1,000; 400,000	GCA	ground control apparatus; Guatemala; system
		GCE	certificate; examination
		GCH	Grand Cross of Hanover
		GCM	greatest common measure
		GCP	good clinical practice
		GCSE	certificate; examination
		GD	gadolinium
		GDC	dentists
		GDE	gourde
		GDNS	gardens; road; street; way
		GDR	German Democratic Republic
GA	gallium; General Assembly; general average; Georgia	GE	General Electric; Georgia; germanium; metalloid
		GEC	company
GAEL	Gaelic	GEL	gelatine
GAL	Galatians; gallon(s); unit	GEN	case; data; dope; general; general information; Genesis; genitive; information; lowdown
GALL	gallon(s)		
GANDS	Gilbert and Sullivan		
GANDT	drink; gin and tonic		
GAR	army; veterans	GENL	general
GAT	killer; weapon	GEO	George
GATT	trade agreement	GEOG	geographic; geographical; geography
GAZ	Garry; Gary; gazette; gazetteer	GEOL	geologic; geological; geology
GB	gigabyte(s); gilbert; Great Britain	GER	German; Germany; gerund; gerundive
GBA	Alderney	GEV	giga-electronvolt(s); unit
GBG	Guernsey	GG	gee-gee; horse; mount
GBH	grievous bodily harm	GH	Ghana; growth hormone
GBJ	Jersey	GHB	designer drug; drug
GBM	Isle of Man; man	GHQ	general headquarters
GBS	dramatist; Shaw	GHZ	gigahertz
GBZ	Gibraltar	GI	general issue; government issue; Joe; soldier
GC	George Cross; Maltese cross		
		GIB	Gibraltar

GIF	file format; graphic interchange format	GPA	grade point average
		GPI	condition; illness
GIFT	fertility treatment; gamete intra-Fallopian transfer; infertility treatment	GPO	General Post Office
		GR	grain; gram(s); gramme(s); Greece; Greek; grey; gross; king; King George; sovereign; weight
GIL	Gilbert		
GIS	computer system; system		
GK	Greek	GRACE	system; telephone system
GKN	company	GRAPO	terrorists
GLA	acid	GRCM	degree; graduate
GLCM	degree; graduate; ground-launched cruise missile; killer; missile; weapon	GRI	George, King and Emperor; king
		GRID	database
GLD	guilder	GRO	grove; road; street; way
GLOS	Gloucestershire	GRT	weight
GM	car manufacturers; Geiger-Müller; Geiger-Müller counter; general manager; General Motors; genetically modified; George Medal; gram(s); gramme(s); grand master; grant-maintained; weight	GRU	Chief Intelligence Directorate; intelligence; intelligence service
		GS	gauss; general secretary; general staff; grammar school; guineas; school
		GSM	grammes per square metre; grams per square metre; school; system; telephone system
GMBH	company; firm; limited company		
		GSO	general staff officer
GMC	doctors; Germanic	GSOH	good sense of humour; great sense of humour
GMO	genetically modified organism	GST	goods and services tax; tax
GNER	lines; railway		
GOC	general	GT	automobile; car; drop; gran turismo; great; gutta
GOM	Gladstone; grand old man		
		GTC	teaching council; trainers
GOP	Grand Old Party; party; Republicans	GTCE; GTCNI; GTCS; GTCW	teaching council
GOSH	hospital	GTD	guaranteed
GOV	government; governor	GTI	automobile; car; gran turismo injection
GP	doctor; Gallup Poll; general practitioner; glory to the Father; graduated pension; Grand Prix; group; healer; race		
		GUI	graphical user interface
		GUM	store
		GUS	Angus; Augustus

G

abbreviation ⇨ full form

GUT	Grand Unified Theory	GW	gigawatt(s); weight
GUY	Guyana	GWR	lines; railway
GVH	graft-versus-host	GY	gray; unit
GVHD	condition; illness	GYM	gymnasium; gymnastic(s); exercise; jerks
GVW	weight		

H	aitch; B natural; bomb; constant; drug; fireplug; gas; hand; hard; hearts; height; henry; heroin; hertz; horse; hospital; hot; hotel; hour; Hungary; husband; hydrant; hydrogen; magnetic field strength; note; Planck's constant; tap; time; two hundred; two hundred thousand; unit; 200; 200,000
HA	guns; hahnium; have; Heavy Artillery; hectare(s); in this year
HAB	Habakkuk
HAG	Haggai
HAL	Henry
HAN	Hannah
HANDC	hot and cold; taps
HANTS	Hampshire
HB	haemoglobin; hard black
HBC	company
HBO	hyperbaric oxygen
HC	Holy Communion; House of Commons; parliament
HCF	forces' chaplain; highest common factor
HCG	drug
HCP	handicap
HD	heavy-duty
HDL	high-density lipoprotein; protein
HDTV	high-definition television; television
HE	ambassador; cardinal; diplomat; explosive(s); gas; governor; helium; high explosive; His Eminence; His Excellency
HEB; HEBR	Hebrew; Hebrews
HER	heir; heraldry
HERO	danger of explosion
HERTS	Hertfordshire
HET	heterosexual
HEX	hexadecimal; uranium hexafluoride
HF	hafnium; half; high frequency
HFC	gas
HG	hectogram(s); Her Grace; His Grace; High German; mercury; weight
HGH	hormone; human growth hormone
HGV	heavy goods vehicle
HH	hands; Her Highness; His Highness; His Holiness; very hard
HI	Hawaii; Hawaiian Islands
HIE	Highland and Islands Enterprise
HIM	Her Imperial Majesty; His Imperial Majesty
HIND	Hindustani
HIST	histology; historian; history
HIV	illness; infection; virus
HK	Hong Kong; House of Keys; Manx parliament; parliament
HKJ	Jordan
HL	hectolitre(s); House of Lords; parliament
HM	harbourmaster; hectometre(s); Her Majesty; His Majesty; Her Majesty's; His Majesty's; king; queen
HMA	high memory area
HMAS; HMCS	ship
HMG	government

HMP	erected this monument; prison	HRE	Holy Roman Emperor; Holy Roman Empire
HMS	ship	HRT	therapy
HMSO	publishers	HS	hassium; high school; Home Secretary; in this sense; school
HMV	record company; record distributor; record shop		
HN	Honduras	HSBC	bank
HNC	certificate; examination	HSE	dwelling; house
HND	diploma	HST	Hawaii Standard Time; high-speed train; train
HO	dwelling; Head Office; holmium; Home Office; hostilities only; house	HT	electricity; half-time; height; high tension
HOLS	holidays; vacation	HTLV	virus
HON	honey; honorary; Honourable; sweetheart	HTM	file format
		HTML	file format; language; programming language
HOS	Hosea	HUD	head-up display
HOTOL	aircraft	HUGO	Human Genome Organisation
HP	half pay; high pressure; high priest; hire purchase; horsepower; Houses of Parliament; legislators; never-never; parliament; sauce; Westminster	HUNG	Hungarian; Hungary
		HV	high voltage
		HW	dismissed; hit wicket
		HWM	high water mark
HPV	virus	HY	Henry
HQ	headquarters	HYP	hypotenuse; hypothesis; hypothetical
HR	Croatia; home rule; hour; House of Representatives; human resources; parliament; personnel; time		
		HZ	hertz; unit

I

I	current; digit; ego; electric current; few, figure; imaginary number; in; independence; independent; India; information; institute; international; iodine; island; isle; Italy; not a lot; me; one; small number; 1	ICI	company; multinational; multinational chemical company
1	first; single; unit; unity	ICR	intelligent character recognition
IA	actuaries; Iowa	ICSH	hormone
IAA	acid	ICSI	fertility treatment; fertilization; infertility treatment
IAL	language; programming language	ICT	information and communication technology
IAS	indicated air speed; instrument approach system; store; system	ICU	hospital department; unit
IB	in the same place; Isabel; Isabella; Isbel; Ishbel; Isobel	ID	I had; I should; Idaho; identification; identity; infectious diseases; information department; inner diameter; intelligence department; intradermal; the same
IBF	boxers		
IBID	in the same place	IDA	Idaho
IBM	company	IDB	illicit diamond buying
IBRD	bank	IDD	dialling
IBS	illness; syndrome	IDE	integrated development environment; integrated drive electronics
IC	circuit; in charge; in command; integrated circuit; internal combustion; managing; ninety-nine; 99	IDP	integrated data processing
		IE	id est; Indo-European; that is; that is to say; that's
ICA	accountants; Institute of Contemporary Arts; Invalid Care Allowance	IEE	engineers
		IF	intermediate frequency
ICBM	killer; missile; weapon	IFA	independent financial adviser
ICC	cricketers	IFP	party
ICD	disc	IFR	instrument flying regulations; instrument flying rules
ICE	electronics; engineers; internal combustion engine	IFS	Irish Free State
		IG	Indo-Germanic
ICHEME	engineers	IGC	intergovernmental conference
		IGN	unknown

IHC; IHS	Jesus Christ
IHT	inheritance tax; tax
II	few; not a lot; small number; two; 2
11	eleven; side
III	few; not a lot; small number; three; 3
IK	Isaac
IKE	Eisenhower; general; Isaac; president
IKY	Isaac
IL	forty-nine; Illinois; Israel; 49
ILL	Illinois; illustrated
ILLIT	illiterate
ILS	instrument landing system; system
IM	I am
IMECHE	engineers
IMF	International Monetary Fund
IMHO	in my humble opinion
IMINE	engineers
IMIT	imitation; imitative
IMO	in my opinion; miners
IMP	emperor; empress; imperial
IMPER	imperative
IMPERF	imperfect
IMPERS	impersonal
IMPGAL; IMPGALL	imperial gallon(s)
IN	fashionable; inch(es); Indiana; indium
INBD	inboard
INC	including; inclusive; incorporated
INCL	including; inclusive
INCOG	under an assumed name; unidentified; unknown
IND	in the name of God; independent; India; Indian; Indiana
INDEF	indefinite
INDIC	indicative
INDIV	individual
INF	below; dope; infantry; inferior; infinitive; informal; information; lowdown
INFIN	infinitive
INFL	influenced
INLA	army; nationalists
INLOC	in its place
INRI	Jesus Christ
INS	inches; insurance
INSET	in-service education and training
INST	instant; institute; institution; present month; this month
INT	interest; interior; internal; international
INTERJ	interjection
INV	designed; devised; he/she designed; he/she devised; invented; invoice
IO	input/output
10	Honour; ten
IOJ	journalists
IOM	Isle of Man; man; Manx
IOU	debt; obligation; promise
IOW	Isle of Wight
IP	Internet Protocol
IPA	advertisers; alphabet; international phonetic alphabet; publishers
IPC	publishers
IPO	initial public offering
IQ	intelligence; intelligence quotient; the same as

IR	infrared; Inland Revenue; Iran; Ireland; iridium; Irish; taxmen	IT	computer studies; computing; drink; information technology; Italian; Italian vermouth; Italy; vermouth; wine
IRA	army; provisional; Republicans		
IRBM	missile; weapon	ITA	alphabet; initial teaching alphabet
IRL	Ireland	ITAL	Italian; italic; Italy
IRQ	Iraq	ITT	company; telephone company
IRREG	irregular; irregularly		
IRS	taxmen	ITV	broadcasters; network
IS	Iceland; income support; independent suspension; information science; information systems; internal security; Isaiah; island(s); isle(s)	IU	international unit; intrauterine
		IUCD	contraceptive
		IUD	contraceptive
		IV	few; four; intravenous; intravenous drip; intravenously; not a lot; small number; 4
ISA	individual savings account; Isabel; Isabella; Isaiah; Isbel; Ishbel; Isobel; savings account		
		IVE	I have
ISBA	advertisers; society	IVF	fertility treatment; fertilization
ISD	dialling		
ISL	island	IVY	Ivor
ISO	film speed; isolated replay	IW	Isle of Wight
ISP	Internet service provider	IX	few; muses; nine; not a lot; small number; 9
1ST	first; principal		

J

J	coat-card; court card; Honour; I; jack; Japan; Jay; joint; joule; journal; judge; Juliet; justice; knave; one; pen; unit; 1	JNR	junior
		JO	Joanna; Joseph; Josepha; Josephine
JA	Jamaica	JOE	GI; Joseph; Josepha; Josephine
JAL	airline		
JAM	Jamaica	JON	Jonah; Jonathan; Jonathon
JAN	Janet; Janice; January; month; weeks	JOS	Joseph
JAP	Japanese	JOSH	Joshua
JC	Jesus Christ; Julius Caesar	JP	justice; Justice of the Peace; magistrate
JCL	language; programming language	JPEG; JPG	file format
		JR	junior
JCS	Joint Chiefs of Staff	JSA	dole; Jobseeker's Allowance
JEM	James	JUD	doctor; judges; Judith
JEN	Jenifer; Jennifer	JUDG	judges
JER	Jeremiah	JUL	July; month; weeks
JET	Joint European Torus	JUN	June; junior; month; weeks
JIM	James	JUNR	junior
JIT	just-in-time	JUV	juvenile
JJ	judges; justices	JY	jansky; July; month

K	Cambodia; carat; catalogue; catalogue of Mozart's works; catalogue of Scarlatti's works; coat-card; constant; court card; grand; great number; heaps; Honour; kalium; kaon; karat; Kay; kelvin; kilo; kilobyte(s); kilometre(s); kina; king; Kirkpatrick; knight; knit; Köchel; krona; króna; krone; kwacha; large number; load(s); lot(s); man; many; Mozart's works; piece; potassium; royalty, ruler; Scarlatti's works; thousand; two hundred and fifty; unit; velocity constant; vitamin; weight; works by Mozart; works by Scarlatti; 250; 1,000; 250,000	KE	kinetic energy
		KEN	Kenneth; Kentucky
		KEV	Kevin; kilo-electronvolt(s)
		KFOR	Kosovo Force; peacekeepers
		KG	keg(s); kilogram(s); kilogramme(s); knight; Knight of the Garter; unit; weight
		KGB	Committee of State Security; police; Soviet secret police
		KGY	kilogray(s)
		KHZ	kilohertz
		KIM	Kimball; Kimberley
		KIT	Catharine; Catherina; Catherine; Christopher; Katharine; Katherine
		KJ	kilojoule(s)
		KL	city; kilolitre(s); Kuala Lumpur
		KLM	airline
KAN	Kansas	KM	kilometre(s); knight
KANS	Kansas	KMH	kilometres per hour; rate
KANU	party	KN	knot(s); nautical measure
KAT	katal; unit	KO	demolish; flatten; floor; kick-off; knock out; knockout; punch; stun
KAY	Catharine; Catherina; Catherine; Katharine; Katherine		
		KP	jankers; kitchen police; knight; police
KB	kilobyte(s); King's Bench; knight; knight bachelor	KPG	kilometres per gallon; rate
KBE	knight	KPH	kilometres per hour; rate
KBYTE	kilobyte	KR	gas; krona; króna; krone; krypton
KBYTES	kilobytes		
KC	Czech koruna; Kennel Club; kilocycle(s); King's Counsel; silk	KS	cancer; condition; illness; Kansas; Kyrgyzstan
KCAL	kilocalorie(s)	KSTJ	knight
KCB; KCMG; KCVO	knight	KT	karat; kiloton(s); kilotonne(s); knight; Knight of the Thistle; knot; man; piece
KD	knocked down; Kuwaiti dinar		

abbreviation ⇨ full form

KU	kurchatovium	KWIC	keyword in context
KV	kilovolt(s)	KWOC	keyword out of context
KW	kilowatt(s)	KWT	Kuwait
KWAC	keyword and context	KY	Kentucky
KWH	kilowatt-hour(s); unit	KZ	Kazakhstan

L	angular momentum; apprentice; beginner; el; elevated railroad; fifty; fifty thousand; hand; heaps; inductance; laevorotatory; lake; lambert; large; large number; Latin; latitude; league; learner; lecturer; left; length; liberal; libra; licentiate; Lima; line; lira; lire; litre(s); live; load(s); loch; long; lot(s); Lough; luminance; Luxembourg; many; molar latent heat; novice; party; plate; pound(s); pound(s) sterling; pupil; railroad; railway; side; sinister; specific latent heat per gramme; student; tiro; tyro; undergraduate; weight; 50; 50,000
LA	city; degree; lane; lanthanum; lawmakers; legislative assembly; legislators; Library Association; Literate in Arts; Los Angeles; Louisiana; note; road; scholar; street; way
LAB	dog; laboratory; labour; Labrador; party; politician
LAC	leading aircraftman; leading aircraftsman
LACW	leading aircraftswoman; leading aircraftwoman
LAH	note
LAM	lamentations
LAMDA	school
LAN	local area network; network
LANCS	Lancashire
LANG	language
LAO	Laos
LAPD	police
LAR	Libya
LAT	gents; lateral; Latin; latissimus dorsi; latitude; muscle; toilet
LAV	gents; toilet
LB	dismissed; extra; leg before; leg bye; Liberia; pound(s); weight
LBC	broadcasters; company
LBF	pound force
LBO	leveraged buyout
LBS	school
LBW	dismissed; leg before wicket
LC	in the place cited; left centre; letter of credit; library; Library of Congress; lower case
LCD	least common denominator; liquid crystal display; lowest common denominator
LCH; LCHIR	surgeon
LCJ	judge; Lord Chief Justice
LCM	least common multiple; lowest common multiple
LCPL	non-commissioned officer
LCST	speech therapist; therapist
LD	Lady Day; lethal dosage; lord; Low Dutch; quarter day
LDC	less developed country
LDG	leading
LDL	protein
LDP	lordship
LDS	dentist; Latter-Day Saints; praise be to God always
LDV	Home Guard
LEA	local education authority

abbreviation ⇨ full form

LECT	lecture; lecturer	LIFO	last in, first out; redundancy order
LED	light-emitting diode		
LEG	lawmakers; legal; legate; legato; legislation; legislative; legislators; legislature	LILO	last in, last out; redundancy order
		LIN	lineal; linear
		LINCS	Lincolnshire
LEGIS	legislation; legislative; legislature	LING	linguistics
		LINN	Linnaean; Linnaeus
LEICS	Leicestershire	LIQ	liquid; liquor
LEIP	Leipzig	LIT	literal; literally; literary; literature
LEM	Lunar Excursion Module; spacecraft		
		LITD	doctor
LEN	Leonard	LITH	Lithuania; Lithuanian; print; printing
LES	Leslie		
LETS	barter system; system; trading system	LITHO	print; printing
		LITHOG	printing
LEV; LEVIT	Leviticus	LITTD	doctor
LEW	Lewis; Louis; Ludovic; Ludovick	LIZ	Elizabeth
		LJ	judge; Lord Justice
LEX	lexicon	LL	language; Late Latin; lines; Lord Lieutenant; Low Latin; shall; will
LF	line feed; low frequency		
LG	language; large; Low German		
		LLA	degree; Lady Literate in Arts; scholar
LGE	large		
LGTH	length	LLCM	musician
LGU	golfers	LLD	doctor
LGV	large goods vehicle	LLM	Master of Laws
LH	hormone; left hand; sinister	LLW	low-level waste
		LM	long metre; Lord Mayor; lumen; lunar module; unit
LHD	doctor; left-hand drive		
LI	light infantry; lithium; Long Island; soldiers; 51		
		LMS	lines; local management of schools; railway
LIB	book; liberal; liberation; librarian; library; party; politician	LN	logarithm; natural logarithm
		LNE; LNER	lines; railway
LIBDEM	party	LNG	fuel; gas
LIBOR	bank rate; rate	LOD	logarithm odds
LIE	loss of independent existence	LOFC	line of communication
		LOG	logarithm
LIEUT	lieutenant	LON	longitude
LIFFE	futures exchange		

LOND	London	LSA	apothecary; chemist
LONDIN	of London	LSD	acid; drug; pounds, shillings and pence; sterling
LONG	longitude		
LONRHO	company		
LOO	gents; toilet	LSE	school
LOQ	speaks	LSI	large-scale integration
LOU	Louisa; Louise	LSO	orchestra
LP	disc; Labour Party; Lady Provost; long-playing; Lord Provost; low pressure; party; record; Socialists	LT	lieutenant; Lithuania; low tension
		LTA	Lawn Tennis Association
		LTD	limited
		LTH	theologian
LPG	fuel; gas	LU	lumen; lutetium
LPM	lines per minute; rate	LV	Latvia; luncheon voucher; meal ticket; 55
LPO	orchestra		
LPOOL	Liverpool	LVO	lieutenant
LPS	Lord Privy Seal	LW	lawrencium; long wave
LR	lawrencium; lira	LWM	low-water mark
LRAM	musician	LWR	light-water reactor
LRCP	doctor	LWT	broadcasters
LRCS	surgeon	LX	electrical(s); lighting technicians; lux; sixty; unit; 60
LRP	fuel		
LS	guinea; in the place of the seal; Lesotho; Linnaean Society; naturalists; society	LXX	Septuagint; seventy; 70
		LXXX	eighty; 80
		LY	Libya; light-year(s)

M	am; Bond's boss; em; fellow; Frenchman; golden arches; great number; heaps; large number; load(s); lot(s); mac; madam; maiden; male; Malta; man; many; mark; married; masculine; mass; master; McDonalds; medium; member; meridiem; metre(s); Metro; midday; Mike; mile(s); million(s); minute(s); Monday; money; monsieur; month(s); motorway; my; noon; road; Scotsman; spymaster; thousand; unit; 1,000; 1,000,000
MA	blood relative; degree; graduate; Massachusetts; Master of Arts; Morocco; mother; relation; relative; scholar
MAC	coat; Jock; multiplex analogue components; Scotsman; waterproof
MACC	Maccabees
MACH	machinery
MAD	mutual assured destruction
MAFF	ministry
MAG	comic; magazine; magnesium; magnetic; magnetism; magnitude; Margaret
MAJ	major
MAL	Malachi; Malaysia
MAM	blood relative; mother; relation; relative
MAN	network
MANDIR	managing director
MANDS	store
MAR	March; memory address register; month; weeks
MARC	machine readable cataloguing
MARG	margin; marginal
MARQ	noble
MAS	masculine
MASH	hospital
MASC	masculine
MASS	Massachusetts
MAT	Mathilda; Matilda; matinée; matrix; Matthew; Matthias
MAX	Maximilian; maximum
MAY	Maria; Marie; Mary
MB	Bachelor of Medicine; doctor; Manitoba; mark; mark of the Beast; mbar(s); meg(s); megabyte(s); millibar(s)
MBA	business course
MBI	management buy-in
MBM	meat and bone meal
MBO	management buy-out
MBYTE	meg(s); megabyte(s)
MC	chair; chairman; chairperson; chairwoman; compère; decoration; host; mac; Master of Ceremonies; medal; Member of Congress; Member of Council; midheaven; Military Cross; Monaco; Scotsman; 1,100
MCB	miniature circuit breaker
MCC	club; cricket club; cricketers
MCH	degree; Master of Surgery; surgeon
MCIJ	journalist
MCP	chauvinist; male chauvinist pig
MCR	middle combination room; middle common room

MCS	megacycles per second; rate	METAL; METALL	metallurgical; metallurgy
MD	doctor; Doctor of Medicine; healer; managing director; Maryland; mendelevium; mentally deficient; Moldova; 1,500	METAPH	metaphor; metaphorical; metaphysical; metaphysics
		METEOR	meteorology
		METI	ministry
MDLLE	mademoiselle; miss	MEV	mega-electronvolt(s)
MDM	madame	MEX	Mexican; Mexico
MDMA	drug; ecstasy; stimulant	MEZ	Central European Time
MDS; MDSC	dentist	MF	machine-finished; medium frequency; mezzo-forte; Middle French; moderately loud; multi-frequency; rather loud; rather loudly
ME	chronic fatigue syndrome; condition; engineer(s); illness; Maine; maître; master; mechanical engineer; Messerschmitt; Methodist Episcopal; Middle East; Middle English; mining engineer; most excellent; note; syndrome		
		MFD	manufactured
		MFH	foxhunter
		MFRS	manufacturers
		MFS	genetic disorder; syndrome
MECH	mechanical; mechanics	MFT	let a mixture be made
MECON	economist	MG	automobile; car; car manufacturers; machine-gun; magnesium; milligram(s); milligramme(s); Morris Garages; weapon; weight
MED	educationalist; medical; medicine; medieval; Mediterranean; medium; middle; sea		
MEG	Margaret		
MEM	member; memorandum; memorial; message; note; remember	MGB	ministry; police
		MGL	Mongolia
		MGLAM	Mid Glamorgan
MEP	lawmaker; legislator; Member of Parliament; parliamentarian; politician; representative	MGM	film studio
		MGR	clergyman; manager; Monseigneur; Monsignor; Monsignore
MESSRS	gentlemen	MHR	representative
MET	metaphor; metaphorical; metaphysical; metaphysics; meteorological; meteorology; metropolitan; Metropolitan Police; opera house; police	MHRA	researchers
		MHZ	megahertz
		MI	intelligence; Michigan; mile(s); military intelligence; note; security agency; spies; 1,001

M

abbreviation ⇨ full form

M1	motorway; road
MIA	absent; missing; unaccounted for
MIC	mica; Micah
MICH	Michaelmas; Michigan
MID	amid; midshipman
MIDAS	missile defence alarm system; system
MIDDX	Middlesex
MIG	aircraft; aircraft designers; fighter; fighter aircraft; warplane
MIL	military
MILIT	military
MIN	clergyman; clergywoman; minimum; minister; ministry; minute(s); mobile identification number; parson; time
MINN	Minnesota
MIPS	millions of instructions per second; rate
MIR	mortgage interest relief
MIRAS	mortgage interest relief
MISC	miscellaneous
MISS	Mississippi
MIT	university
MIZ	miserable; misery
MJ	megajoule(s)
MK	Macedonia; mark; markka
MKS	metre-kilogram-second
MKSA	unit
MKT	market
ML	mile(s); millilitre(s); 1,050
MLD	mean lethal dose
MLF	multilateral force
MLLE	Frenchwoman; mademoiselle; miss

MM	Frenchmen; gentlemen; messieurs; military medal; millimetre(s); 2,000
MME	Frenchwoman; madame
MMI	man-machine interaction; man-machine interface
MMM	company
MMOL	millimole(s)
MMR	measles, mumps and rubella; vaccination; vaccine
MMUS	musician
MN	manganese; Merchant Navy; Minnesota; sailors
MND	condition; illness
MNR	marine nature reserve
MO	doctor; magneto-optical; Maureen; medical officer; method of working; Missouri; modus operandi; molybdenum; moment; money order; month; second; time
MOC	Mozambique
MOD	ministry; moderate; moderate speed; moderato; modern; Whitehall warriors; youth
MOH	doctor; ministry
MOL	mole; unit
MOLWT	molecular weight
MOM	blood relative; mother; relation; relative
MOMA; MOMI	museum
MON	day; Monday; Monmouthshire
MONSIG	clergyman; Monsignor; Monsignore
MONT	Montana; Montgomeryshire

abbreviation ⇨ full form

M

MOR	Morocco; music	MRSA	bacteria; bacterium; bug; hospital bug; resistant bacterium; superbug
MORI	pollsters; researchers		
MOS	metal oxide semiconductor; months	MS	condition; degree; draft; illness; manuscript; Master of Surgery; Mauritius; millisecond(s); Mississippi; screed; surgeon
MOT	certificate; test		
MOU	memorandum of understanding		
MP	commoner; fairly quiet; lawmaker; legislator; melting-point; Member of Parliament; Metropolitan Police; mezzo-piano; military police; moderately quiet; moderately softly; mounted police; mounties; municipal police; parliamentarian; police; politician; redcap; representative		
		MSA	motorway service area
		MSB	most significant bit
		MSC	degree; graduate; scientist
		MSDOS®	disc operating system; computer operating system; system
		MSG	flavour enhancer
		MSGR	clergyman; Monsignor; Monsignore
		MSL	mean sea-level
		MSM	anti-inflammatory agent
MPC	computer	MSP	Member of Parliament; parliamentarian; politician; representative
MPG	miles per gallon; rate		
MPH	miles per hour; rate		
MPHARM	pharmacist	MSS	manuscripts
MPHIL	degree; philosopher	MSV	millisievert(s)
MPS	chemist; pharmacist; philologist	MSW	social worker
		MT	mean time; mechanical transport; meitnerium; metical; Montana; mount; mountain; Mountain Time
MR	Master of the Rolls; Mauritian rupee; Mister; motivation research; motivational research		
MRA	Moral Rearmament	MTB	boat
MRBM	killer; missile; weapon	MTD	detector; moving target detector
MRCA	aircraft; fighter aircraft; warplane		
		MTH	month
MRCP	doctor	MTV	music television; television
MRE	meal(s) ready to eat		
MRG	Minority Rights Group	MU	micron
MRI	hospital department; medical specialism; scan	MUD	computer game
		MUFTI	Minimum Use of Force Tactical Intervention
MRPHARMS	pharmacist		
MRS	Mistress; wife		

MUM	blood relative; chrysanthemum; flower; mother; relation; relative	MVP	most valuable player
		MW	Malawi; medium wave; megawatt
MUS	museum; music; musical	MWF	doctors
MUSB	degree; musician	MX	maxwell; Middlesex; missile experimental; 1,010
MUSD	doctor; musician		
MV	boat; megavolt(s); mendelevium; merchant vessel; motor vessel; muzzle velocity; ship; 1,005	MY	boat; motor yacht; yacht
		MYA	Myanmar
		MZM	metical
MVD	Soviet Ministry of Internal Affairs		

N	and; cardinal point; direction; en; gas; infinite; innumerable; knight; man; midday; naira; name; National; nationalist; navy; neuter; neutral; neutron; new; newton(s); ngultrum; ninety; ninety thousand; nitrogen; nominative; noon; Norse; north; northern; Norway; note; noun; November; nuclear; number; opponent; part of London; partner; piece; player; point; pole; quarter; unit; unknown number; unsexy; way; 90; 90,000	NAT	born; National; Nathan; Nathaniel; national; nationalist; native; natural
		NATO	North Atlantic Treaty Organization
		NATS	National Air Traffic Services
		NAU	Nauru
		NAUT	nautical
		NAV	naval; navigable; navigation; navigator; net asset value
		NB	mark; mark well; Nebraska; New Brunswick; niobium; no-ball; North Britain; North British; nota bene; note well; observe; remember; take notice
NA	Netherlands Antilles; North America; not applicable; not available; sodium		
NACL	salt	NBA	basketball association; boxers; Net Book Agreement
NAD	coenzyme; nicotine patch	NBC	broadcasters; company; network; nuclear, biological and chemical
NAFTA	trade agreement		
NAH	Nahum	NC	computer; free; National Curriculum; network computer; no charge; North Carolina; numerical control
NAHT	head teachers; teachers		
NAI	injury; non-accidental injury		
NAM	Namibia; Vietnam	NCC	consumer council; curriculum council; Nature Conservancy Council
NAN	Ann; Anna; Anne; blood relative; grandmother; Hannah; relation; relative		
NAND	circuit	NCEA	certificate
NANDQ	Notes and Queries	NCO	corporal; non-commissioned officer; sergeant-major
NAO	National Audit Office		
NAP	card game; napoleon		
NAPO	probation officers	NCP	National Car Parks
NAS	academy; National Academy of Sciences; Noise Abatement Society; society	NCT	childbirth trust; National Childbirth Trust
		ND	neodymium; no date; North Dakota; not dated

NDAK	North Dakota	NGO	non-governmental organization
NE	corner; direction; gas; locality; Nebraska; neon; New England; north-east; north-eastern; opponents	NGR	Nigeria
		NH	New Hampshire
		NHI	National Health Insurance
NEB	Bible; Nebraska	NHS	health service
NEBR	Nebraska	NI	national insurance; nickel; North Island; Northern Ireland; Six Counties; Ulster
NEC	exhibition centre		
NED	Edgar; Edmund; Edward; Edwin		
NEDC	economic development council	NIC	national insurance contributions; newly industrialized country; Nicaragua
NEF	energy foundation; National Energy Foundation		
		NICE	National Institute for Clinical Excellence
NEG	negative; negatively; negotiable	NIH	National Institutes of Health
NEH	Nehemiah		
NEL	engineering laboratory; National Engineering Laboratory	NIX	nothing doing
		NJ	New Jersey
NEMCON; NEMDISS	all agreed; unanimous	NK	killer; natural killer
		NL	it is not clear; it is not permitted; The Netherlands; not far
NEP	Nepal		
NES	eczema society; society	NLC	lottery regulator
NETH	The Netherlands	NLP	natural language processing; neurolinguistic programming
NEUT	neuter; neutral		
NEV	Nevada		
NF	fascists; language; Newfoundland; no funds; Norman French; Northern French; party	NM	nanometre(s); nautical measure; nautical mile; New Mexico
		NMC	Nursing and Midwifery Council
NFER	educational researchers		
NFL	football league	NMEX	New Mexico
NFS	fire service; National Fire Service; not for sale	NMR	nuclear magnetic resonance
NFT	film theatre; National Film Theatre	NNE	direction; north-north-east; one o'clock
NFU	farmers		
NG	duff; National Guard; no good; rotten	NNI	Noise and Number Index
		NNP	net national product
NGC	New General Catalogue		

NNW	direction; north-north-west	NS	nanosecond(s); new series; New Style; nielsbohrium; non-smoker; not specified; Nova Scotia; nuclear ship; partners
NO	natural order; New Orleans; nobelium; Norway; not out; number		
NOC	National Olympic Committee; Olympic committee	NSA	security agency
		NSAID	drug
NODE	dictionary	NSC	safety council
NO1	best; first; lieutenant	NSF	not sufficient funds; science foundation
NOM	case; nominal; nominative	NSRA	rifle association
NONSEQ	non sequitur	NSU	illness; infection; non-specific urethritis
NOP	pollsters; researchers		
NOR	circuit; Norman; north; Norway; Norwegian; nucleolar-organizing region	NSW	New South Wales
		NT	Bible; books; collection of books; conservationists; holy books; National Theatre; National Trust; New Testament; no trumps; Northern Territory; Northwest Territories; preservationists; religious book(s); scripture; trust
NORM	normal; Norman		
NORTHANTS	Northamptonshire		
NORTHUMB	Northumberland		
NOS	numbers		
NOT	circuit		
NOTTS	Nottinghamshire	NTA	award
NOV	month; November; weeks	NTH	north
NOX	nitrogen oxide	NTP	normal temperature and pressure
NP	neptunium; new paragraph; New Providence; no place; Notary Public; noun phrase	NTS	conservationists
		NTWT	net weight
		NU	name unknown; ngultrum
NPA	publishers		
NPG	portrait gallery	NUC	nuclear
NPL	physics laboratory	NUI	university
NPV	net present value	NUJ	journalists
NR	near	NUM	miners; number; numbers; numeral
NRA	rifle association; rivers authority; shooters	NUMB	numbers
		NUR	railwaymen
NRV	net realizable value	NUS	students
		NUT	teachers

NV	Nevada; new version	NY	city; New York
NVCJD	condition; illness; infection	NYC	New York City
		NYE	Aneirin; Aneurin
NVD	no value declared	NYO; NYOS	orchestra
NW	corner; direction; locality; north-west; north-western; Northwest Territories; opponents; part of London	NYPD	police
		NYSE	New York Stock Exchange
		NZ	dominion; Kiwi; New Zealand
NWS	North Warning System; system; system of radar stations		

O

O	ball; blob; blood group; cipher; circle; circuit; circular letter; descendant of; disc; duck; egg; eleven; eleven thousand; examination; gas; Henry; hoop; hug; level; loop; love; naught; nil; no; nothing; nought; of; Ohio; old; omega; omicron; on; ordinary; Oscar; ought; oval; oxygen; ring; round; spangle; zero; zilch; zip; 0; 11; 11,000
OA	on account of
OAM	midnight
OAP	elder; old-age pensioner; senior citizen
OAS	on active service; Organization of American States; Organization of French Settlers
OAU	Organization of African Unity; unionists
OB	by the way; dead; deceased; departed; died; former pupil; old boy; Order of the Bath; out of bounds; outside broadcast
OBAD	Obadiah
OBDT	obedient
OBE	Order of the British Empire
OBJ	case; object; objective
OBL	oblique; oblong
OBS	obscure; observation; obsolete
OC	commanding officer; Officer Commanding; Officer in Charge; only child; Order of Canada; original cover; overcharge
OCD	illness; obsessive-compulsive disorder
OCF	Forces' chaplain
OCR	examination board; optical character reader; optical character reading; optical character recognition
OCT	autumn; fall; month; octavo; October; weeks
OCTU	Officer Cadet Training Unit; unit
OD	Officer of the Day; ordnance data; ordnance datum; overdose; overdraft; overdrawn; surfeit
ODA	Overseas Development Administration
ODI	one-day international
OE	language; oersted; Old English
OED	dictionary; lexicon
OEIC	company; open-ended investment company
OEM	original equipment manufacturer
OER	over
OF	language; Oddfellow; Old French
OFCOM	Office of Communications
OFF	officer; official; officinal
OFFER	electricity regulator's office
OFM	Franciscans; minor friars; monks
OFT	fair trading office; regulators
OFTEL	telecommunications office

OGPU	force; police; special government political administration	OOP	object-oriented programming
OH	Ohio	OP	Dominican(s); friar(s); insecticide; killer; monk(s); observation point; observation post; old penny; operation; operator; opposite; opposite prompt; opus; order; Order of Preachers; organophosphate; out of print; work
OHG	language; Old High German		
OHMS	On Her/His Majesty's Service		
OHP	overhead projector		
OIC	oh, I see		
OILC	Offshore Industry Liaison Committee		
OK	all correct; all right; approval; approve; certainly; endorse; endorsement; fair; fine; jake; moderate; okay; Oklahoma; Roger; sanction; satisfactory; yes	OPCIT	in the work cited
		OPE	open
		OPP	oppose; opposed; opposite
		OPS	operations; operations officer; operations room; other people's
		OPT	optative; optic; optical; optimum; optional; very well indeed
OKE	certainly	OPW	public works office
OKLA	Oklahoma	OR	circuit; men; operational research; operations research; Oregon; other ranks; researchers; soldiers
OLAF	European Anti-Fraud Office		
OLE	object linking and embedding		
OM	distinction; Old Measurement; Order of Merit	ORCH	orchestra; orchestrated by
		ORD	ordained; order; ordinary; ordnance
OME	manpower economics office	OREG	Oregon
OMOV	one member one vote; system; voting system	ORIG	origin; original; originally
		ORR	rail regulator's office
OMR	optical mark recognition	ORT	oral rehydration therapy; therapy
ON	language; Old Norse; Ontario		
ONC	certificate; examination	OS	blue jacket; extra large; fat; great; huge; jumbo; large; map-makers; Old Style; operating system; ordinary seaman; Ordnance Survey; osmium; outsize; sailor; salt; very large
OND	diploma		
ONO	or near offer; or nearest offer		
ONS	national statistics office		
OO	glasses; offers over; pair; spectacles		

OSA	Augustinian(s); hermit friar(s); monk(s); order	OTC	Officers' Training Corps; over the counter
OSB	Benedictine(s); friar(s); monk(s); order	OTE	on-target earnings
		OTT	excessive; excessively; over the top; too much
OSF	Franciscan(s); friar(s); monk(s); order	OU	Open University; Oxford University; university
OSP	died without issue		
OSS	strategic services office	OUP	press; publishers
OT	Bible; books; collection of books; holy books; hospital department; medical specialism; occupational therapist; occupational therapy; Old Testament; religious book(s); scripture; therapist; therapy	OXON	of Oxford; Oxfordshire
		OZ	Australia; lightweight; ounce(s); weight
		OZS	ounces

P	clergyman; clergywoman; coin; constant; copper; four hundred; four hundred thousand; king's son; leaf; man; page; papa; parking; parson; participle; pascal; pastor; pawn; pedal; pee; pence; penny; peseta; peso; phosphorus; piano; piece; Portugal; positive; power; president; pressure; priest; prince; probationary driver; provisional driver; pula; purl; queen's son; quiet; soft; unit; 400; 400,000
PA	assistant; blood relative; dad; each year; father; old man; Panama; pascal; past; Pennsylvania; per annum; personal appearance; personal assistant; press; Press Association; protactinium; public address; public address system; publicity agent; Publishers Association; relation; relative; unit
PABA	acid
PABX	exchange; telephone exchange
PAC	Pan-Africanist Congress
PACE	Police and Criminal Evidence Act
PAD	horse
PAIN	Parents Against Injustice
PAK	Pakistan; Pakistani
PAL	broadcasting system; phase alternation line
PAM	Pamela
PAMR	public access mobile radio; radio
PANAM	airline
PANDO	company; shipping line
PANDP	post and packing; postage and packing
PAP	past participle
PAR	paragraph; parallel; parish
PARA	paragraph; paratrooper
PARL	parliament; parliamentary
PAS	acid; drug
PASOK	party; Socialists
PASS	passive
PAT	past tense; patent; patented; Patricia; Patrick; planned activities time; teachers
PATH; PATHOL	pathological; pathology
PAX	exchange; private automatic exchange; telephone exchange
PAYE	pay as you earn
PB	lead; paperback; Pharmacopoeia Britannica; Plymouth Brethren
PBIT	profit before interest and tax
PBX	exchange; telephone exchange
PC	computer; constable; Parish Council; per cent; personal computer; police constable; police officer; political correctness; politically correct; postcard; privy councillor
PCB	pollutant
PCC	parochial church council; Press Complaints Commission; watchdog
PCE	piece

PCI	peripheral component interconnect
PCM	per calendar month; pulse code modulation
PCN	telephone network
PCP	anaesthetic; analgesic; condition; drug; fungicide; illness; infection; killer
PCR	politically correct retailing; polymerase chain reaction
PCS	principal clerk of session
PCT	per cent
PCV	passenger-carrying vehicle
PD	paid; palladium; police; police department
PDA	personal digital assistant
PDF	file format; portable document format
PDI	pre-delivery inspection
PDL	language; page description language; programming language
PDQ	as soon as possible
PE	church; drill; exercise(s); gymnastics; jerks; Peru; physical education; potential energy; price-earnings ratio; Prince Edward Island; Protestant Episcopal
PEC	muscle
PED	pedestrian
PEG	Margaret
PEME	pulsed electro magnetic energy
PEN	gaol; jail; Penelope; peninsula; penitentiary; prison; writers
PENN	Pennsylvania

PEP	personal equity plan; political and economic planning; savings scheme
PER	period; person
PERAN	each year; per annum
PERH	perhaps
PERMIL	by the thousand; each thousand
PERPRO	by proxy; by the agency of another
PERS	Persian; person
PERT	programme evaluation and review technique
PES	peseta
PET	brain scanner; lubricant; Peter; plastic; potentially exempt transfer; scan; scanner; thermoplastic; tomography
PF	Patriotic Front; pfennig; pianoforte; procurator fiscal
PFA	footballers
PFC	private first class
PFD	personal flotation device
PFI	Private Finance Initiative
PFLP	liberationists
PFP	Partnership for Peace
PG	classification; film classification; guest; lodger; parental guidance; paying guest; Portugal; Portuguese
PGA	golfers
PGM	past grand master
PH	acidity; alkalinity; drug; local; pub; Public House; purple heart; stimulant
PHAB	physically handicapped and able bodied
PHAR	pharmaceutical
PHARM	drugs; pharmaceutical

PHB	polymer	PL	language; library; place; plural; Plymouth; Poet Laureate; Poland; programming language; public library
PHD	degree; doctor; graduate; philosopher		
PHI	permanent health insurance		
PHIL	Philadelphia; Philippians; philological; philology; philosophical; philosophy	PLA	Port of London Authority; Pre-School Learning Alliance; river authority
PHILEM	Philemon	PLC	company; firm; limited company; public company; public limited company
PHON; PHONET	phonetics		
PHONOG	phonography	PLO	liberationists
PHOT	photographic; photography	PLP	party; Socialists
		PLR	public lending right
PHR	phrase	PLU	plural
PHYS	physician; physics; physiology	PLUP	pluperfect
		PLUR	plural
PI	detective; eye; pious; private investigator; religious	PM	after death; afternoon; cabinet maker; leader; lunchtime; past master; post meridiem; post mortem; postmaster; premium; prime minister; promethium; provost marshal
PIA	airline; Personal Investment Authority		
PIBS	permanent interest-bearing share; share		
PIC	film; picture	PMBX	telephone exchange
PICS	pictures	PMDD	illness
PID	condition; illness; infection	PMG	Paymaster General; Postmaster General
PIM	personal information manager	PMO	doctor; principal medical officer
PIN	personal identification number	PMR	paymaster
		PMS	syndrome
PINX	he/she painted; painted	PMT	photomechanical transfer; premenstrual tension; tension
PIP	Philip; Phillip		
PIX	pictures		
PJS	pyjamas	PN	IOU; promissory note
PK	pack; Pakistan; park; peak; peck; psychokinesis	PNA	acid; Palestinian National Authority; peptide nucleic acid
PKU	illness		
		PND	depression; illness; postnatal depression

PNDB	perceived noise decibel	PPC	picture postcard; prospective parliamentary candidate; to take leave
PNG	Papua New Guinea; portable network graphic		
PO	chamberpot; humourless; metalloid; petty officer; pilot officer; pole; polonium; post office; postal order; sailor; stolid	PPE	course; philosophy, politics and economics
		PPI	plan position indicator
		PPM	parts per million
		PPP	pianississimo; Private Patients' Plan; public private partnership
POA	Prison Officers' Association		
POD	pay on delivery; tripod	PPS	additional postscript; Parliamentary Private Secretary; Parliamentary Secretary; third thoughts
POLECON	political economy		
POM	dog; English person; prisoner of Mother England		
		PQ	Province of Quebec
POP	blood relative; dad; father; persistent organic pollutant; point of presence; poppet; popular; popularly; population; post office preferred; relation; relative	PR	clergyman; clergywoman; couple; pair; parson; per; praseodymium; present; press release; price; priest; prince; prize ring; proportional representation; Provençal; public relations; Puerto Rico; through the rectum
POS	point of sale; position; positive		
POST	point of sale terminal; power-on-self-test	PREB	prebend; prebendary
		PREF	preface; preference; preferred
POT	drug; potentiometer; rheostat		
		PREP	preparation; preposition
POTS	plain old telephone system; system; telephone system	PRES	present; president
		PRIN	principal
		PRN	as the need arises
POV	point of view		
POW	captive; hostage; prisoner	PRO	archive; expert; hustler; professional; prostitute; Public Record Office; public relations officer; whore
PP	by proxy; by the agency of another; clergyman; clergywoman; for and on behalf of; leaves; pages; parish priest; parson; past participle; past president; per pro; pianissimo; postage and packing; present pupil; proxy; very soft; weak		
		PROB	likely; probable
		PROF	academic; chair; chairman; chairperson; chairwoman; professor
PPA	Pre-School Playgroups Association	PROM	memory; store

abbreviation ⇨ full form

PROP	Preservation of the Rights of Prisoners; proper; properly; property; proposition; proprietor	PT	drill; exercise(s); gymnastics; jerks; Pacific Time; part; past; past tense; personal trainer; personal training; physical therapy; physical training; pint(s); platinum; point; port; postal telegraph; post-town; pupil teacher; purchase tax; tax; therapy; unit
PROT	Protestant		
PROTEM	for the time being		
PROV	Provence; proverbs; provincial; provost		
PROX	next month		
PRP	performance-related pay; profit-related pay	PTA	Parent-Teacher Association; Passenger Transport Authority; peseta
PRS	Performing Rights Society; President of the Royal Society; society	PTE	Passenger Transport Executive; private
PRT	tax	PTFE	plastic
PRU	company	PTO	please turn over; public telecommunications operator
PS	afterthought; codicil; file format; footnote; horsepower; Pharmaceutical Society; pharmacists; Philological Society; police officer; police sergeant; postscript; private secretary; prompt side; psalm; psalms; second thoughts; society; supplement; underwrite	PTSD	illness
		PTY	proprietary
		PU	pick-up; plutonium; pulled up
		PUB	local
		PUD	afters; dessert; sweet
		PULV	powder
PSA	antigen; pleasant Sunday afternoon; Property Services Agency; Public Services Authority	PUP	dog
		PVA	resin
		PVC	plastic
		PVFS	syndrome
PSC	passed staff college	PVS	permanent vegetative state; persistent vegetative state
PSEUD	nom de plume; pen-name		
PSL	private sector liquidity	PW	per week; policewoman
PSNI	police	PWA	person with AIDS
PSS	packet switching system; system	PWD	public works department
		PWR	pressurized water reactor
PST	Pacific Standard Time	PWS	syndrome
PSTN	network; telephone network	PWT	pennyweight
		PX	shop; store
PSV	public service vehicle	PY	Paraguay
PSW	psychiatric social worker; social worker	PYO	pick-your-own

Q	coat-card; court card; cue; drug; electric charge; fever; five hundred; five hundred thousand; Honour; man; piece; poser; Qatar; quality; quart; quarter; quarto; Quebec; queen; Queensland; query; question; quetzal; quintal; royalty; ruler; ship; trichosanthin; 500; 500,000
QA	quality assurance
QADS	quality assurance data system; system
QALY	quality-adjusted life year
QB	Queen's Bench
QC	quality circle; quality control; Queen's College; Queen's Counsel; silk
QCD	quantum chromodynamics
QED	quantum electrodynamics; which was to be proved
QEF	which was to be done
QEH	Queen Elizabeth Hall
QEI	which was to be found
QIC	quarter-inch cartridge
QID	four times a day
QL	as much as you please; language; programming language; query language; quintal
QLD	Queensland
QM	quartermaster
QMC	hospital
QPR	football club; football team
QQV	which see
QR	quarter
QS	sufficient quantity
QSO	quasar; quasi-stellar object
QT	amount; quantity; quart; quiet; secret
QTO	quarto
QTOL	aircraft
QTS	qualified teacher status
QTY	amount; quantity
QU	poser; quart; quarter; quarterly; queen; question
QUAR	quart; quarter; quarterly
QUE	Quebec
QUOT	quotation
QV	as much as you wish; which see
QY	query

R	arithmetic; classification; constant; eighty; eighty thousand; film classification; flower; gas constant; hand; king; man; piece; queen; radius; rand; reading; Réaumur's thermometric scale; recipe; rector; Regina; republic; resistance; restricted; Rex; right; river; Robert; Romania; Romeo; Röntgen unit; rook; root; rouble; rule; run; runner; runs; rupee; side; starboard; take; unit; writing; 80; 80,000	RAH	hurrah
		RAID	disks; redundant array of independent disks; redundant array of inexpensive disks
		RALL	becoming gradually slower; gradually slowing; slowing gradually
		RAM	academy; memory; musicians; relative atomic mass; Royal Academy of Music; school
RA	academician; academy; Argentina; artillery; artist(s) Burlington House; gunner(s); illness; limner; painter; radium; rear admiral; rheumatoid arthritis; Royal Academician; Royal Academy (of Arts); Royal and Ancient; Royal Artillery; soldiers; unit	RAMC	doctors
		RAN	navy; Royal Australian Navy; sailors; service
		RANDA	club
		RANDR	rest and recreation; rest and relaxation
		RAS	astronomers
		RAVC	veterinary surgeons
		RAX	telephone exchange
		RAY	note; Rachael; Rachel; Raymond
RAAF	airmen; service	RB	Botswana; Rifle Brigade; rubidium; soldiers
RAB	Butler; Robert		
RABB	rabbinical	RBI	run batted in
RAC	club; corps; drivers; driving club; motorists	RC	Catholic; Christian; church; Red Cross; Roman Catholic; Taiwan
RAD	heater; radian; radiator; radical; radius; unit		
		RCA	academy; broadcasters; Central African Republic; Royal Canadian Academy; Royal College of Art
RADA	academy; Royal Academy of Dramatic Art; school		
RADAR	Royal Association for Disability and Rehabilitation		
		RCAF	airmen; Royal Canadian Air Force; service
RADC	dentists	RCB	Congo: Republic of
RAE	Rachael; Rachel; Raymond	RCC	church; Roman Catholic Church
		RCD	residual current device
RAF	air force; airmen; force; Royal Air Force; service	RCGP	doctors; general practitioners

RCH	Chile	REC	company; receipt; recipe; record; recreation; recreation ground; regional electricity company; take
RCM	musicians; regimental court martial		
RCMP	police		
RCN	navy; nurses; Royal Canadian Navy; service	RECD	received
		RECPT	receipt
RCO	organists	RECT	clergyman; clergywoman; parson; rector; rectory
RCP	doctors		
RCR	radiologists	REF	judge; referee; reference
RCS	scientists; signallers; surgeons	REFCH	church; Reformed Church
RCT	drivers; transporters	REFL	reflection; reflective; reflex; reflexive
RCVS	veterinary surgeons		
RD	clergyman; clergywoman; Dean; parson; refer to drawer; reserve decoration; road; rural dean; rutherford; street; way	REG	Reginald; registration number
		REGD	registered
		REGT	regiment
		REHAB	hospital department; medical specialism; rehabilitate; rehabilitation; rehabilitation centre
RDA	recommended daily allowance; recommended dietary allowance		
RDC	rural development council	REL	related; relating; relation; relative
RDF	detector; fuel; radio direction finder; radio direction finding	RELD	relative density
		REM	rapid eye movement; sleep
RDS	radio data system; system	REME	corps; engineers
RDX	cyclonite; explosive; research department explosive	REP	agent; repeat; repertory; repetition; representative; reprobate; republic; Republican; reputation; salesman; saleswoman
RE	about; again; are; church; concerning; divinity; engineer(s); in connection with; note; on; Reformed Episcopal; regarding; religious education; rhenium; Royal Engineers; rupee; sapper(s); touching; with regard to; with respect to		
		REPR	reprint; reprinted
		REPT	receipt; report
		RES	research; reservation; reserve; residence; resolution; Royal Economic Society; society
		RET	keep; retain; retired; return
REAU	Réaumur's thermometric scale		
		RETD	retired; returned

abbreviation ⇨ full form

REV	clergyman; clergywoman; father; parson; Revelation of St John; Reverend; revise; revised; revision; vicar	RIAS	architects; Architectural Association
		RIBA	architects; Architectural Association
REVD	clergyman; clergywoman; parson; Reverend	RIC	chemist; police
		RICS	surveyors
REVVER	Revised Version	RIE	recognized investment exchanges
REX	Reginald		
REZ	reservation	RIGS	regionally important geological site
RF	French Republic; radio frequency; rutherfordium	RIM	Mauritania
		RIO	city; port
RFA	auxiliaries; sailors	RIP	epigraph; epitaph; rest in peace
RFC	airmen; rugby footballers		
RFS	Register of Friendly Societies	RISC	computer; reduced instruction set computer
RFU	rugby footballers	RIT	becoming gradually slower; gradually slowing; ritenuto; slowing gradually
RG	Guinea		
RGG	guards		
RGN	nurse		
RGS	geographers	RJE	remote job entry
RGT	regiment	RJET	remote job entry terminal
RGV	remote guidance vehicle	RKO	film studio
RH	Haiti; Rhesus; Rhesus factor; rhodium; right hand; Royal Highness	RL	game; Lebanon; library; reference library; Rugby League
RHA	artillery; regional health authority; Royal Horse Artillery; soldiers	RLC	logisticians
		RLO	returned letter office
		RLS	Stevenson
RHET	rhetoric	RLY	railway
RHG	guards	RM	British troops; jollies; jolly; leatherneck; Madagascar; marine(s); postal service; ream; resident magistrate; room; Royal Mail; Royal Marines
RHS	gardeners; historians; horticulturalists		
RI	divinity; Indonesia; King and Emperor; Queen and Empress; religious instruction; religious teaching; Rhode Island; Royal Institution; water colourist		
		RMA; RMAS	Sandhurst; school
		RMI	Retail Motor Industry Federation
RIA	radioimmunoassay	RMM	Mali
RIAM	musicians; school	RMN	nurse

RMO	resident medical officer	RP	church; condition; illness; Philippines; portrait painters; Received Pronunciation; Reformed Presbyterian; Regius Professor; retinitis pigmentosa
RMP	police		
RMS	liner; meteorologists; root mean square		
RN	force; gas; main force; navy; Niger; nurse; radon; registered nurse; Royal Navy; sailors; Senior Service; service		
		RPB	recognized professional body
RNA	acid; ribonucleic acid(s)	RPC	Rail Passengers' Council; watchdog
RNAS	naval air service; naval air station	RPG	language; programming language; report program generator; role-playing game
RNIB	institute for blind people		
RNID	institute for deaf people		
RNLI	lifeboat institution	RPI	retail price index
RNR	naval reserve; reservists	RPM	rate; resale price maintenance; retail price maintenance; revolutions per minute
RNVR	reservists; volunteers		
RO	dismissed; recto; Romania; run out		
ROB	Robert	RPN	reverse Polish notation
ROC	corps; observers	RPO	orchestra
ROD	Roderick; Rodney	RPR	party
ROH	opera house	RPS	photographers; rate; revolutions per second
ROK	Korea; South Korea		
ROM	memory; roman; Romans	RPT	repeat; report; turner
ROO	animal; boxer; hopper; Joey; jumper	RPV	remotely-piloted vehicle
		RR	automobile; bishop; car; car manufacturers; clergyman; clergywoman; Right Reverend; roller; Rolls-Royce®
ROS	Rosalind; Rosamond; Rosamund		
ROSPA	accident preventers		
ROT	occupational therapist; therapist	RRP	recommended retail price
		RS	Royal Society; rupees; society
ROU	Uruguay		
ROV	remotely-operated vehicle	RSA	academy; artists; Returned Services Association; school; South Africa
ROZ	Rosalind; Rosamond; Rosamund		
		RSAMD	school
		RSC	chemistry society; company; players; society

abbreviation ⇨ full form

RSI	injury; Relative Strength Index; repetitive strain injury; repetitive stress injury; strain; stress	RTF	file format; rich text format
		RTHON	Right Honourable
		RTPI	town planners
RSJ	beam; girder; joist	RTREV	clergyman; clergywoman; Right Reverend
RSL	literature society; Returned Services League; society	RTZ	company; mining company
RSM	medical society; musicians; non-commissioned officer; regimental sergeant major; San Marino; school	RU	Burundi; game; Rugby Union; ruthenium
		RUC	police
		RUR	play
		RUS	Russia
RSNC	conservationists; preservationists	RV	Bible; recreational vehicle; rendezvous; Revised Version
RSNO	orchestra		
RSPB	bird protectors; conservationists; preservationists; protectionists	RW	Right Worshipful; Right Worthy
		RWA	Rwanda
		RWS	artists
RSV	Bible; Revised Standard Version	RWY	railway
		RY	line(s); railway; transport system
RT	radio telegraphy; radio telephony; right		
		RYA; RYS	sailors
RTA	accident; road traffic accident	RZS; RZSE	zoologists
RTD	retired		
RTE	broadcasters; Irish Radio and Television		

S	bend; cardinal point; direction; dollar; entropy; good man; good woman; has; holy man; holy woman; is; opponent; partner; player; point; pole; quarter; Sabbath; saint; schilling; second(s); section; seven; seventy; seventy thousand; shilling; siemens; sierra; singular; small; society; son(s); soprano; south; southern; spades; special; square; stokes; strangeness; succeeded; sulphur; sun; Sunday; Sweden; unit; us; way; 7; 70; 70,000	SAL	antiquaries; Sara; Sarah
		SALT	Strategic Arms Limitation Talks; Strategic Arms Limitation Treaty
		SAM	killer; missile; rocket; Samuel; uncle; weapon
		SAN	hospital; sanatorium
		SANDL	savings and loan; savings and loan association
		SANDM	sadomasochistic; sexual practices
		SANDT	signalling and telecommunications
		SANS; SANSK	language; Sanskrit
		SAR	detector; search and rescue
SA	according to art; antiquaries; appeal; army; brown shirts; company; glamour; it; limited company; Nazi terrorist militia; oomph; Salvation Army; Saudi Arabia; save; sex appeal; society; Society of Antiquaries; Society of Arts; South Africa; South America; South Australia; storm section; storm troopers; terrorists; without date	SARS	illness; infection; superbug; virus
		SARSAT	emergency detection system; system
		SAS	antiquaries; commandos; paramilitary; Special Air Service
		SAT	day; Saturday; scholastic aptitude test; standard assessment task
		SATB	soprano, alto, tenor, bass
		SAW	surface acoustic wave
SAB	saboteur	SAX	musical instrument
SABC	broadcasters	SAYE	save as you earn
SAC	arts council; Scottish Arts Council; special area of conservation; Strategic Air Command	SB	antimony; metalloid; substantive
		SBN	standard book number
SACN	nutritionists	SBS	sick building syndrome; Special Boat Service; syndrome
SAD	depression; illness; seasonal affective disorder		
SAE	engineers; stamped addressed envelope		
SAFR	South Africa; South African		

SC	certificate; examination; he/she sculptured; ie; in other words; namely; police officer; scandium; School Certificate; sculptured; self-catering; self-contained; Signal Corps; signallers; small capitals; South Carolina; special constable; that is; that is to say	SDP	party; social, domestic and pleasure; Socialists
		SDR; SDRS	special drawing rights
		SE	corner; direction; engineers; home counties; Kent; locality; metalloid; opponents; part of London; selenium; south-east; south-eastern
SCAN; SCAND	Scandinavian	SEA	Single European Act
SCANMAG	defamation	SEAC	South-East Asia Command
SCBU	hospital department		
SCD	doctor	SEAQ	Stock Exchange Automated Quotations
SCE	certificate; examination	SEATO	treaty organization
SCF	Save the Children Fund	SEC	function; function of an angle; secant; second; secretary; Securities and Exchange Commission; time
SCH	schilling; school		
SCI	science; scientific		
SCID	condition		
SCIFA	scire facias; writ		
SCIL; SCIZ	in other words; namely; to wit	SECAM	broadcasting system; French TV broadcasting system
SCL	student of civil law		
SCM	midwife; Student Christian Movement	SECH	function; function of an angle; hyperbolic secant
		SECREG	according to rule
SCODA	drug abuse conference	SECT	section
SCOT	Scotland; Scottish	SECY	secretary
SCP	protein	SED	education department
SCR	scruple; senior combination room; senior common room	SEM	course; electron microscope; microscope; semester; semicolon; seminary; Semitic; term
SCRIPT	scripture	SEN	nurse; senate; senator; senior; senza; special education needs
SCULP; SCULPT	he/she sculptured; sculptor; sculpture; sculptured		
		SEO	executive officer; senior executive officer
SD	sine die; South Dakota; Swaziland; without date	SEP	month; separate; September; weeks
SDAK	South Dakota		
SDI	Star Wars; Strategic Defense Initiative	SEPT	month; September; weeks
		SEQ	following
SDLP	party; Socialists		

SER	serial; series; serine; sermon	SHT	sheet(s)
		SHTG	shortage
SERG; SERGT	non-commissioned officer; sergeant	SI	international system; metalloid; note; scientific system of units; silicon; South Island; system
SERPS	pension scheme		
SESS	session		
SET	secure electronic transaction	SIB	blood relative; brother; relation; relative; Securities and Investments Board; sibling; sister
SETI	search for extraterrestrial intelligence		
SETS	Stock Exchange Electronic Trading Service; trading service		
		SIDS	syndrome
SF	party; science fiction; sforzando; sforzato; signal frequency; Sinn Fein; with sudden emphasis	SIG	signature; signor; signore; special interest group
		SIM	evangelical; Simeonite; Simon
		SIN	function; function of an angle; sine
SFA	footballers; nothing at all; Securities and Futures Authority; sweet Fanny Adams	SING	singular
		SINH	function; function of an angle; hyperbolic sine
		SIPP	pension
SFO	Serious Fraud Office	SIR	Ecclesiasticus; Wisdom
SFX	special effects; suffix	SIS	blood relative; girl; honey; relation; relative; satellite information services; Secret Intelligence Service; security agency; Security Intelligence Service; sibling; sister
SFZ	sforzando; sforzato; with sudden emphasis		
SG	seaborgium; Solicitor-General; specific gravity		
SGD	signed		
SGML	language; programming language		
SGP	Singapore	SJ	Jesuit(s)
SGT	non-commissioned officer; sergeant	SJC	Supreme Judicial Court
		SK	Saskatchewan; Slovakia
		SKR; SKT	language; Sanskrit
SH	second-hand; shorthand; used	SL	serjeant-at-law; solicitor; solicitor at law
SHA	Strategic Health Authority	SLBM	missile; weapon
		SLD	party; sailed
SHF	superhigh frequency	SLO	Slovenia
SHM	simple harmonic motion	SLR	camera; weapon
SHPT	shipment	SLT	therapist
SHR	share(s)		

SM	non-commissioned officer; sadomasochism; samarium; sergeant-major; sexual practices; short metre	SOS	appeal; distress signal; help; signal; urgent appeal
SMD	surface-mounted device	SOT	stay-on-tab
SME	enterprise; Suriname	SOV	coin; sovereign
SMM	Holy Mother Mary	SP	childless; odds; special; species; spelling; starting price; without issue
SMO	doctor; senior medical officer		
SMS	short message service	SPA	special protection area
SN	according to nature; Senegal; tin	SPAB	conservationists; preservationists; protectionists
SNCF	railway		
SNG	gas	SPAD	signal passed at danger
SNO	nurse; senior nursing officer	SPD	party
		SPECIF	specific; specifically
SNP	nationalists; party	SPET	scanner
SNR	senior	SPF	sun protection factor
SO	note; seller's opinion; shipping order; signal officer; Somalia; south; special order; staff officer; standing order	SPG	special patrol group
		SPGR	specific gravity
		SPL	Scottish Premier League
		SPP	species
		SPR	sapper
SOC	socialist; society	SPUC	anti-abortionists; protectionists
SOE	Special Operations Executive		
		SPVOL	specific volume
SOFS	Song of Solomon; Song of Songs	SQ	following; square
		SQA	Scottish Qualifications Authority
SOH	note		
SOHO	small office/home office	SQL	language; programming language
SOL	note; solicitor; Solomon; solution		
		SQN	squadron
SOLGEN	Solicitor-General	SQUID	interference device
SOLR	solicitor	SR	lines; railway; senior; señor; sir; sister; Southern Region; steradian; strontium; unit
SOM	Somerset		
SOP	cohabitee; cohabiter; partner; significant other person; soprano		
		SRA	Strategic Rail Authority
SOR	sale or return	SRAM	memory; store
		SRC	Student Representative Council

SRCH	chiropodist	START	Strategic Arms Reduction Talks; Strategic Arms Reduction Treaty
SRN	nurse		
SRO	self-regulatory organization; standing room only	STAT	immediately
		STC	subject to contract
SS	bodyguard; force; Nazi élite corps; police; Protective Squad; saints; Schutzstaffel; screw steamer; ship; steamer; steamship	STD	condition; dialling; illness; infection; sexually transmitted disease; standard; subscriber trunk dialling; venereal disease
SSA	standard spending assessment	STE	good woman; holy woman; Sainte
SSC	society; Society of the Holy Cross; Solicitor before the Supreme Courts	STEN	gun; killer; weapon
		STEP	Special Temporary Employment Programme
SSD	department; Most Holy Lord; Pope	STER	sterling
		STG	sterling
SSE	direction; south-south-east	STH	south
		STOL	aircraft
SSL	secure sockets layer	STP	professor of theology; standard temperature and pressure; theologian
SSM	killer; missile; weapon		
SSN	standard serial number		
SSP	statutory sick pay; subspecies	STR	steamer; straight; strong
		STUC	Scottish Trades Union Congress
SSPP	subspecies		
SSR	Soviet Socialist Republic	STV	broadcasters; single transferable vote
SSRI	antidepressant; drug		
SST	Concorde; supersonic transport	SUB	advance; journalist; lieutenant; loan; press employee; subaltern; subeditor; subject; sublieutenant; submarine; subscriber; subscription; subsistence money; substitute; U-boat
SSVC	broadcasters		
SSW	direction; south-south-west		
ST	dismissed; good man; good person; good woman; hast; holy man; road; saint; São Tomé and Príncipe; stone; strait; street; stumped; way; weight		
		SUBJ	case; subject; subjective; subjunctive
		SUBS	subscription
		SUBST	substantive; substitute
STA	station	SUD	Sudan
STAFFS	Staffordshire	SUDS	syndrome

abbreviation ⇨ full form

SUE	Susan; Susanna; Susannah; Susanne; Suzanna; Suzannah; Suzanne	SWA	South-West Africa
		SWALK	sealed with a loving kiss
		SWAPO	party
SUN	day; Sunday	SWAT	police; special weapons and tactics
SUP	above; superfine; superior; superlative; supine; supplement; supreme	SWG	standard wire gauge
		SW1	Westminster
		SWL	safe working load
SUPCT	superior court; supreme court	SWOT	analysis; strengths, weaknesses, opportunities and threats
SUPP; SUPPL	supplement		
SUPR	supreme	SWP	party; Socialists
SUPT	superintendent	SWRI	Scottish Women's Rural Institute
SURF	fuel		
SURG	surgeon; surgery; surgical	SY	Seychelles; Surrey
SUS	Susan; Susanna; Susannah; Susanne; Suzanna; Suzannah; Suzanne	SYL	syllable; syllabus
		SYM	symbol; symmetrical; symphony; symptom
		SYN	synonym; synthetic
SUV	sport utility vehicle	SYND	syndicate
SV	Holy Virgin; sievert(s); under that heading; under the voice; under the word; unit; Your Holiness	SYNOP	summary
		SYR	Syria
SVGA	super video graphics array		
SW	corner; Cornwall; direction; locality; opponents; part of London; short wave; small women; small women's; south-west; south-western		

T	bone; cart; hundred and sixty; hundred and sixty thousand; it; junction; model; plate; shirt; square; surface tension; tango; tare; tee; temperature; tenor; tense; tesla; Thailand; the; time; to; ton(s); transitive; tritium; troy; unit; 160; 160,000
TA	army; force; irregulars; reservists; tantalum; Territorial Army; unit; volunteers
TAB	drug; tablet; tabulate; tabulator; Totalizator Agency Board; vaccine
TAFE	technical and further education
TAI	International Atomic Time
TAM	cap; television audience measurement; Thomas
TAN	function; function of an angle; tangent
TANH	function; function of an angle; hyperbolic tangent
TAR	blue jacket; sailor; salt; tarpaulin
TAS	Tasmania
TASM	killer; missile; weapon
TASS	news agency
TAT	pony
TAVR	army
TB	boat; condition; consumption; illness; infection; terabyte(s); terbium; torpedo boat; tuberculosis
TBA	to be advised
TBC	to be confirmed
TBSP	tablespoon; tablespoonful
TBT	fungicide; killer

TC	technetium
TCA	tricarboxylic acid cycle
TCD	dictionary; lexicon; *The Chambers Dictionary*; Trinity College, Dublin
TCH	Chad
TCM	traditional Chinese medicine; Trinity College of Music, London
TCP	germicide; transmission control protocol
TD	deputy to the Dáil; Member of Parliament; parliamentarian; politician; representative; technical drawing; Territorial Decoration
TE	Lawrence; metalloid; note; tellurium
TEC	detective; police officer; Training and Enterprise Council
TECH	technical; technology
TED	Edward; Heath; Theodore; youth
TEFL	Teaching English as a Foreign Language
TEL	telephone; telephone number
TEM	electron microscope; microscope; transmission electron microscope
TEMP	in the time of; temperature; temporal; temporary
TEN	tenuto
TENN	Tennessee
TENS	stimulation
TER; TERR	terrace; Territory
TES	educational paper; journal; magazine; periodical; supplement; weekly

TESL	Teaching English as a Second Language	TLC	sympathetic treatment; tender loving care
TESOL	Teaching English to Speakers of Other Languages	TLS	journal; literary paper; magazine; periodical; supplement; weekly
TESSA	savings account	TM	thulium; transcendental meditation; Turkmenistan
TEST	testament		
TEUT	Teutonic	TMS	stimulation
TEX	Texas	TN	Tennessee; tradename; Tunisia
TG	Togo; transformational grammar		
		TNF	tumour necrosis factor
TGV	high-speed train; train	TNT	company; dynamite; explosive; high explosive
TH	thorium; Thursday		
THD	doctor; theologian	TO	tax officer; telegraph office; transport officer; turn over
THEAT	theatre; theatrical		
THEOL	theologian; theological; theology		
		TOAT	exact; exactly
THESS	Thessalonians	TOB	Tobit
THI	temperature-humidity index	TOC	company; train operating company
THU; THUR; THURS	day; Thursday	TOCH	society; Talbot House
		TOE	theory of everything
TI	note; titanium	TOM	book; Thomas; volume
TIA	transient ischaemic attack	TON	Tonga
		TP	township; troop
TIB	Isabel; Isabella; Isbel; Ishbel; Isobel	TPI	tax and prices index
		TPR	teleprinter; trooper
TID	three times a day	TR	transactions; transitive; translator; transpose; trustee; Turkey
TIF; TIFF	file format		
TIM	Timothy; traditional Indian medicine		
		TRANS	transitive; translated; translation
TINA	inevitable; inevitably; there is no alternative		
		TRANSF	transfer
TIR	International Road Transport	TREAS	treasurer
		TRH	Their Royal Highnesses
TIT	Titus	TRIN	trinity
TJ	Tajikistan	TSB	bank
TKO	technical knockout	TSE	condition; illness
TL	thallium	TSO	town sub-office
TLA	three-letter acronym	TSP	teaspoon; teaspoonful; textured soya protein

TSR	terminate and stay resident	TUE; TUES	day; Tuesday
TSS	syndrome	TUX	jacket; tuxedo
TT	abstainers; avoiding drink; dry; motor race; non-drinker(s); on the wagon; race; Rechabite; sober; teetotal; teetotallers; Tourist Trophy; Trinidad and Tobago; tuberculin tested	TV	box; cross-dresser; television; transvestite; tube
		TWA	airline
		TWOC	car theft; stealing a car; taking without owner's consent
		TX	Texas
TTL	through the lens	TXT	file format
TTP	trusted third party	TYP; TYPO	typographer; typography
TU	trade union; Tuesday; workers	TYR	tyrosine
TUC	Trades Union Congress; workers		

U

U	bend; boat; certificate; classification; fashionable; film classification; for all to see; hairpin; high-class; posh; privileged; society; trap; tube; uniform; union; unionist; united; universal; Universalist; university; upper class; uranium; Uruguay	UEY	turn; U-turn
		UF	church; United Free Church
		UFC	Universities Funding Council
		UFF	Ulster Freedom Fighters
		UFO	flying saucer; mystery; saucer; unidentified flying object
UA	Ukraine	UHF	ultra-high frequency
UAE	United Arab Emirates	UHT	cream; milk; ultra-heat treated; ultra-high temperature
UAR	United Arab Republic		
UBR	rate; uniform business rate	UJD	doctor
UC	capital; capital letters; University College; upper case	UK	British; United Kingdom
		UKE	musical instrument
		ULA	uncommitted logic array
UCAS	Universities and Colleges Admissions Service	ULCC	boat; ship; tanker; ultra-large crude carrier
UCATT	construction workers	ULF	ultra-low frequency
UCCA	Universities Central Council on Admissions	ULT	last; last month; ultimate; ultimately; ultimo
UCH	hospital	UMIST	university
UCI	cyclists; International Cycling Union	UMP	referee; umpire
UDA	Ulster Defence Association	UMTS	communication system; system; third-generation mobile communications system
UDC	Universal Decimal Classification		
UDF	anti-apartheid groups; United Democratic Front	UN	peacekeepers; United Nations
UDHR	Universal Declaration of Human Rights	UNA	United Nations Association
UDI	declaration; Unilateral Declaration of Independence	UNI	university
		UNICEF	United Nations Children's Fund
UDM	miners	UNIT	Unitarian
UDR	soldiers; Ulster Defence Regiment	UNIV	university
		UNO	United Nations Organization
UDT	United Dominions Trust		
UEA	university	UOM	Myanmar

UP	church; Presbyterian; United Presbyterian	USO	United Service Organizations
UPI	publishers	USP	unique selling point; unique selling proposition
UPS	uninterruptible power supply		
UPVC	double-glazing	USS	ship
URC	church; United Reformed Church	USU	usually
		USW	and so forth; ultrashort waves; ultrasonic waves
URI	illness; infection		
URL	uniform resource locator	UT	do; doh; note; Universal Time; Utah
URU	Uruguay		
US	America; American; as above; no good; Uncle Sam; under-secretary; United Service(s); United States; United States of America; unserviceable; useless	UTC	Universal Time Co-ordinated
		UTD	united
		UTDICT	as said
		UTE	truck; utility truck; utility vehicle
		UTSUP	as above
USA	America; American; army; service; Uncle Sam; United States; United States of America	UU	party; Ulster Unionist; unionists
		UV	light; sunlight; ultraviolet
USAF	air force; airmen; service	UVA; UVB; UVC; UVR	ultraviolet radiation
USB	bus		
USDAW	shopworkers	UWB	ultra-wideband
USGA	golfers	UWIST	university
USM	unlisted securities market	UX	Dutch; wife
USN	navy; service	UZ	Uzbekistan

V

V	against; book; day; dent; digit; few; figure; five; handful; not a lot; see; sign; small number; unit; vanadium; Vatican; Vatican City; vatu; vee; velocity; verb; verse; verso; versus; very; Victor; victory; vide; volt(s); volume; 5; 5,000	VET	animal doctor; doctor; ex-serviceman; old soldier; veteran; Veterinary Surgeon
		VETSURG	animal doctor; Veterinary Surgeon
VA	museum; Vicar Apostolic; vice-admiral; Victoria and Albert; Virginia	VF	video frequency; voice frequency
		VFM	value for money
VAC	cleaner; holiday; vacation	VG	very good; Vicar General
VAD	Voluntary Aid Detachment; volunteer nurses	VGA	video graphics array
		VHF	very high frequency
VAL	valentine; Valerie	VI	few; half-a-dozen; not a lot; six; small number; Vancouver Island; Vehicle Inspectorate; verb intransitive; Violet; Virgin Islands; 6
VAN	advantage; caravan; vanguard		
VANDA	museum	V1	doodlebug; missile; rocket; weapon
VAR	value-added reseller; variable; variant; variety		
		VIC	clergyman; clergywoman; vicarage; Victor; Victoria
VARLECT	variant reading		
VAT	tax; value-added tax	VICE	vice-chancellor; vice-president
VB	verb		
VC	vice-chancellor; Victoria Cross	VID	sixpence; video
		VII	few; not a lot; seven; small number; 7
VCR	recorder		
VCT	venture capital trust	VIII	eight; few; not a lot; small number; 8
VD	condition; fivepence; illness; infection; sexually transmitted disease; venereal disease		
		VIL; VILL	village
		VIP	big cheese; cheese; dignitary; eminence; sixpence; somebody; very important person
VDU	screen; unit; visual display unit		
VE	day; have	VIPS	top brass
VEG	vegetable(s); vegetate	VIR	Victoria, Empress and Queen
VEN	clergyman; clergywoman; venerable	VIS; VISC	viscount
		VIV	Vivian; Vivien; Vivyan
VESA	Video Electronics Standards Association	VIZ	namely; to wit
		VJ	day; video jockey
		VL	variant reading

VMD	doctor
VMI	vertical motion index
VN	Vietnam
VO	left; verso
VOA	broadcasters; Voice of America
VOC	case; vocative
VOCAB	vocabulary
VOD	video-on-demand
VOL	book; volume; voluntary; volunteer
VP	fivepence; vice-president
VPL	visible panty line
VR	Queen Victoria; variant reading; virtual reality
VRAM	memory
VREV	clergyman; clergywoman; Very Reverend
VRI	Victoria, Queen and Empress
VRML	language; programming language
VS	against; versus; Veterinary Surgeon
VT	vatu; verb transitive; Vermont
VTOL	aircraft
VTR	recorder
VUL	Vulgate
VULG	vulgar; Vulgate
VV	verses; vice versa; volumes
VW	automobile; Beetle; car; car manufacturers; Very Worshipful; view; Volkswagen
VYV	Vyvian; Vyvyan

W	cardinal point; direction; Dutch; opponent; part of London; partner; player; point; quarter; tungsten; unit; watt; way; weak; week; weight; Welsh; west; western; whiskey; white; wicket; wide; width; wife; with; wolfram; wolframium; women; women's; won	WEU	Western European Union
		WF	wrong fount
		WG	doctor; Grace; Grenada; water gauge; wire gauge
		WHO	World Health Organization
		WI	West Indies; Wisconsin; Women's Institute(s)
		W1	Mayfair; West End
WA	wall; Washington; West Africa; Western Australia	WIGORN	of Worcester
		WILTS	Wiltshire
WAAC	army; auxiliaries	WIMP	computer interface; weakly interacting massive particles; windows, icons, mouse and pointer
WAAF	air force; auxiliaries		
WAG	The Gambia; Writers and Artists Guild		
WAIS	wide area information server(s)	WIN	Winifred
WAL	Sierra Leone; Walloon	WINTON	of Winchester
WAN	network; wide area network	WIS; WISC	Wisconsin
		WISP	Internet service provider; WAP Internet service provider
WAP	Wireless Application Protocol		
WAR	Warwickshire	WK	time; week; work
WASH	Washington	WL	St Lucia
WATCH	Women and the Church	WM	William
WB	weber	WML	language; programming language
WBA; WBC; WBO	boxers	WN	opponents
WC	gents; part of London; toilet; water closet; West Central; West End; without charge	WNW	direction; west-north-west
		WO	walkover; War Office; Warrant Officer
WD	Dominica; wheel-drive; Works Department	WOO	Beethoven's works; catalogue of Beethoven's works; works by Beethoven
WDA	development agency		
WEA	Workers' Educational Association	WORCS	Worcestershire
		WORM	disc; write once read many times
WED; WEDS	day; Wednesday		
WEF	with effect from	WOW	waiting on weather
WES	Wesley		
WET	Western European Time		

WP	Warsaw Pact; weather permitting; word processing; word processor; Worship; Worshipful	WS	dramatist; opponents; Samoa; Shakespeare; the Bard; Western Samoa; Writer to the Signet
WPB	wastepaper basket	WSW	direction; west-south-west
WPC	constable; policewoman	WT	weight
WPFL	Worshipful	WTO	World Tourism Organization; World Trade Organization
WPM	rate; words per minute		
WR	Western Region	WV	St Vincent and the Grenadines; West Virginia
WRAAC	army		
WRAAF	air force		
WRAC	army; auxiliaries	WWW	network; world wide web
WRAF	air force; auxiliaries	WY	road; street; way; Wyoming
WRANS	navy		
WRP	party	WYO	Wyoming
WRT	with regard to; with respect to		

X	axis; by; Christ; chromosome; classification; co-ordinate; cross; ex; extra; few; figure; film classification; kiss; smacker; ten; ten thousand; times; unknown; variable; vote; without; wrong; 10; 10,000	YAR	Yemen
		YB	ytterbium
		YC	Young Conservative(s)
		YD	yard(s)
		YDS	yards
		YEO	yeomanry
		YHA	hostel; Youth Hostels Association
XC	ninety; 90	YN	yen
XD	ex dividend	YOP	Youth Opportunities Programme
XE	gas; xenon	YORKS	Yorkshire
XI	eleven; players; side; 11	YR	time; year; younger; your
XII	dozen; twelve; 12	YRS	years; yours
XIX	nineteen	YT	that; Yukon Territory
XL	extra large; forty; outsize; very large; 40	YTD	year to date
		YTS	Youth Training Scheme
XM	Christmas	YU	Yugoslavia
XML	extensible mark-up language; language; programming language	YV	Venezuela
XMS	extended memory section	Z	atomic number; axis; bend; contraction; co-ordinate; final; final character; final letter; impedance; izzard; last; two million; two thousand; unknown; variable; Zambia; zed; zee; zenith; zero; zone; Zulu; 2,000; 2,000,000
XN	Christian		
XT	Christ		
XTIAN	Christian		
XV	fifteen; players; side; 15		
XWD; XWORD	crossword		
XX	twenty; 20	ZA	South Africa
XXL	extra extra large	ZB	for example; for instance; say
XXX	thirty; 30		
		ZEPH	Zephaniah
Y	axis; catapult; chromosome; co-ordinate; fork; hostel; hundred and fifty; hundred and fifty thousand; unknown; variable; wye; Yankee; yard; year; yen; young; yttrium; 150; 150,000	ZETA	zero-energy thermonuclear apparatus
		ZEV	zero-emission vehicle
		ZIFT	fertility treatment
		ZL	zloty
		ZN	zinc
		ZR	zirconium

ZRE	Congo: Democratic Republic of; Zaire	ZW	Zimbabwe
ZST	Zone Standard Time	ZZ	sleep; snore; snoring

APPENDICES

Armed Services

AA	LI	RAOC	RM	TAVR
AAC	MP	RAUXAF	RMP	UDR
AC	OCTU	RAVC	RN	US
ACE	OR	RB	RNAS	USA
ANZAC	OTC	RCAF	RNR	USAF
ATC	PMFAFNS	RCN	RNVR	USN
ATS	QARANC	RCS	RNZAF	WRAAC
AVR	QARNNS	RCT	RNZN	WRAAF
BAOR	RA	RE	ROC	WRAC
BEF	RAAF	REME	ROTC	WRAF
BMATT	RAC	RFA	SAC	WRANS
CCF	RADC	RFC	SAS	WRNS
ETS	RAEC	RGG	SBS	
FAA	RAF	RHA	SC	
JCS	RAMC	RHF	SHAEF	
KFOR	RAN	RLC	TA	

Books of the Bible

The list includes Books of the Law, Historical Books, Books of Poetry and Wisdom, Books of the Prophets, the Gospels and Acts, the Epistles or Letters and the Apocrypha.

BAR	ESD	IS	MATT	ROM
BELANDDR	ESTH	ISA	MIC	SAM
CH	EX	JAS	NAH	SIR
CHRON	EXOD	JER	NEH	SOFS
COL	EZ	JON	NUM	SUS
COLOSS	EZEK	JOSH	NUMB	THESS
COR	GAL	JUD	OBAD	TIM
DAN	GEN	JUDG	PET	TIT
DEUT	HAB	LAM	PHIL	TOB
ECCL	HAG	LEV	PHILEM	WISD
ECCLES	HEB	LEVIT	PROV	ZECH
ECCLUS	HEBR	MACC	PS	ZEPH
EPH	HOS	MAL	REV	

Appendices

Chemical Elements

Symbols for both current and former element names are listed. Metallic elements are marked *.

AC*	CO*	I	NP*	SE
AG*	CR*	IN*	NS	SG*
AL*	CS*	IR*	O	SI
AM*	CU*	K*	OS*	SM*
AR	DB*	KR	P	SN*
AS	DY*	KU	PA*	SR*
AT	ER*	LA*	PB*	TA*
AU*	ES*	LI*	PD*	TB*
B	EU*	LR*	PM*	TC*
BA*	F	LU*	PO*	TE
BE*	FE*	LW*	PR*	TH*
BH*	FM*	MD*	PT*	TI*
BI*	FR*	MG*	PU*	TL*
BK*	GA*	MN*	RA*	TM*
BR	GD*	MO*	RB*	U*
C	GE	MT*	RE*	V*
CA*	H	N	RF*	W*
CB*	HA	NA*	RH*	XE
CD*	HE	NB*	RN	Y*
CE*	HF*	ND*	RU*	YB*
CF*	HG*	NE	S	ZN*
CL	HO*	NI*	SB*	ZR*
CM*	HS*	NO*	SC*	

Colleges

CAE	PSC	RCN	RCPS	TCD
CAT	QC	RCNM	RCR	TCM
CFE	RCA	RCO	RCS	UC
CTC	RCGP	RCOG	RCSLT	
HC	RCM	RCP	RCVS	

Counties of England and Wales

BEDS	CUMB	LEICS	SOM
BERKS	DORS	LINCS	STAFFS
BUCKS	DUR	MGLAM	WAR
CAERNS	GLOS	MON	WILTS
CAMB	HANTS	MONT	WORCS
CAMBS	HERTS	NORTHANTS	YORKS
CARDS	IOW	NORTHUMB	
CHES	IW	NOTTS	
CORN	LANCS	OXON	

Countries

Country	ISO country code	Internet suffix	IVR code	Currency	Currency abbreviation	ISO currency code
Afghanistan	AFG	.af	AFG	afghani	Af	AFN
Albania	ALB	.al	AL	lek	Lk	ALL
Algeria	DZA	.dz	DZ	Algerian dinar	AD, DA	DZD
Andorra	AND	.ad	AND	euro	€	EUR
Angola	AGO	.ao	–	kwanza	Kz	AOA
Antigua and Barbuda	ATG	.ag	–	East Caribbean dollar	EC$	XCD
Argentina	ARG	.ar	RA	peso	$	ARS
Armenia	ARM	.am	AM	dram	Drm	AMD
Australia	AUS	.au	AUS	Australian dollar	$A	AUD
Austria	AUT	.at	A	euro	€	EUR
Azerbaijan	AZE	.az	AZ	manat	–	AZM
The Bahamas	BHS	.bs	BS	dollar	BA$, B$	BSD
Bahrain	BHR	.bh	BRN	dinar	BD	BHD
Bangladesh	BGD	.bd	BD	taka	TK	BDT
Barbados	BRB	.bb	BDS	dollar	BD$	BBD
Belarus	BLR	.by	BY	rouble	BR	BYR
Belgium	BEL	.be	B	euro	€	EUR

Appendices

Country	ISO country code	Internet suffix	IVR code	Currency	Currency abbreviation	ISO currency code
Belize	BLZ	.bz	BZ	dollar	BZ$	BZD
Benin	BEN	.bj	DY	CFA franc	CFAFr	XOF
Bhutan	BTN	.bt	–	ngultrum	Nu	BTN
Bolivia	BOL	.bo	BOL	boliviano	$b	BOB
Bosnia and Herzegovina	BIH	.ba	BIH	convertible marka	KM	BAM
Botswana	BWA	.bw	BW	pula	P	BWP
Brazil	BRA	.br	BR	real	R$	BRL
Brunei	BRN	.bn	BRU	dollar	B$	BND
Bulgaria	BGR	.bg	BG	lev	Lv	BGN
Burkina Faso	BFA	.bf	BF	CFA franc	CFAFr	XOF
Burundi	BDI	.bi	RU	franc	BuFr, FBu	BIF
Cambodia	KHM	.kh	K	riel	CRI	KHR
Cameroon	CMR	.cm	CAM	CFA franc	CFAFr	XAF
Canada	CAN	.ca	CDN	dollar	C$, Can$	CAD
Cape Verde	CPV	.cv	–	escudo caboverdiano	CVEsc	CVE
Central African Republic	CAF	.cf	RCA	CFA franc	CFAFr	XAF
Chad	TCD	.td	TCH	CFA franc	CFAFr	XAF
Chile	CHL	.cl	RCH	peso	Ch$	CLP
	CHN	.cn	–	renminbi yuan	RMBY, $, Y	CNY
Colombia	COL	.co	CO	peso	Col$	COP
Comoros	COM	.km	–	franc	KMF	KMF
Congo	COG	.cg	RCB	CFA franc	CFAFr	XAF
Congo, Democratic Republic of the	COD	.cd	ZRE	franc	CF	CDF
Costa Rica	CRI	.cr	CR	colón	CR₡	CRC
Côte d'Ivoire	CIV	.ci	CI	CFA franc	CFAFr	XOF
Croatia	HRV	.hr	HR	kuna	Kn	HRK
Cuba	CUB	.cu	C	peso	Cub$	CUP
Cyprus	CYP	.cy	CY	pound	C£	CYP

Country	ISO country code	Internet suffix	IVR code	Currency	Currency abbreviation	ISO currency code
Czech Republic	CZE	.cz	CZ	koruna	Kč	CZK
Denmark	DNK	.dk	DK	krone	Dkr	DKK
Djibouti	DJI	.dj	–	franc	DF, DjFr	DJF
Dominica	DMA	.dm	WD	East Caribbean dollar	EC$	XCD
Dominican Republic	DOM	.do	DOM	peso	RD$, DR$	DOP
East Timor	TLS	.tp	–	US dollar	$, US$	USD
Ecuador	ECU	.ec	EC	US dollar	$, US$	USD
Egypt	EGY	.eg	ET	pound	£E, LE	EGP
El Salvador	SLV	.sv	ES	colón	¢	SVC
Equatorial Guinea	GNQ	.gq	–	CFA franc	CFAFr	XAF
Eritrea	ERI	.er	–	nakfa	Nfa	ERN
Estonia	EST	.ee	EST	kroon	KR	EEK
Ethiopia	ETH	.et	ETH	birr	EB	ETB
Fiji	FJI	.fj	FJI	dollar	F$	FJD
Finland	FIN	.fi	FIN	euro	€	EUR
France	FRA	.fr	F	euro	€	EUR
Gabon	GAB	.ga	G	CFA franc	CFAFr	XAF
The Gambia	GMB	.gm	WAG	dalasi	D	GMD
Georgia	GEO	.ge	GE	lari	GEL	GEL
Germany	DEU	.de	D	euro	€	EUR
Ghana	GHA	.gh	GH	cedi	¢	GHC
Greece	GRC	.gr	GR	euro	€	EUR
Grenada	GRD	.gd	WG	East Caribbean dollar	EC$	XCD
Guatemala	GTM	.gt	GCA	quetzal	Q	GTQ
Guinea	GIN	.gn	RG	franc	GFr	GNF
Guinea-Bissau	GNB	.gw	RGB	CFA franc	CFAFr	XOF
Guyana	GUY	.gy	GUY	dollar	G$	GYD
Haiti	HTI	.ht	RH	gourde	G, Gde	HTG

Appendices

Country	ISO country code	Internet suffix	IVR code	Currency	Currency abbreviation	ISO currency code
Honduras	HND	.hn	–	lempira	L, La	HNL
Hungary	HUN	.hu	H	forint	Ft	HUF
Iceland	ISL	.is	IS	króna	IKr, ISK	ISK
India	IND	.in	IND	rupee	Re, Rs	INR
Indonesia	IDN	.id	RI	rupiah	Rp	IDR
Iran	IRN	.ir	IR	rial	Rls	IRR
Iraq	IRQ	.iq	IRQ	dinar	ID	IQD
Ireland	IRL	.ie	IRL	euro	€	EUR
Israel	ISR	.il	IL	shekel	IS	ILS
Italy	ITA	.it	I	euro	€	EUR
Jamaica	JAM	.jm	JA	dollar	J$	JMD
Japan	JPN	.jp	J	yen	Y, ¥	JPY
Jordan	JOR	.jo	HKJ	dinar	JD	JOD
Kazakhstan	KAZ	.kz	KZ	tenge	–	KZT
Kenya	KEN	.ke	EAK	shilling	Ksh	KES
Kiribati	KIR	.ki	–	Australian dollar	$A	AUD
Korea, North	PRK	.kp	–	won	NKW	KPW
Korea, South	KOR	.kr	ROK	won	W	KRW
Kuwait	KWT	.kw	KWT	dinar	KD	KWD
Kyrgyzstan	KGZ	.kg	KS	som	Kgs	KGS
Laos	LAO	.la	LAO	kip	Kp	LAK
Latvia	LVA	.lv	LV	lat	Ls	LVL
Lebanon	LBN	.lb	RL	pound	LP, L£	LBP
Lesotho	LSO	.ls	LS	loti	M, LSM	LSL
Liberia	LBR	.lr	LB	dollar	L$	LRD
Libya	LBY	.ly	LAR	dinar	LD	LYD
Liechtenstein	LIE	.li	FL	Swiss franc	SFr, SwF	CHF
Lithuania	LTU	.lt	LT	litas	Lt	LTL
Luxembourg	LUX	.lu	L	euro	€	EUR
Macedonia	MKD	.mk	MK	denar	D, den	MKD
Madagascar	MDG	.mg	RM	ariary	A	MGA

Country	ISO country code	Internet suffix	IVR code	Currency	Currency abbreviation	ISO currency code
Malawi	MWI	.mw	MW	kwacha	MK	MWK
Malaysia	MYS	.my	MAL	ringgit	M$	MYR
Maldives	MDV	.mv	–	rufiyaa	MRf, Rf	MVR
Mali	MLI	.ml	RMM	CFA franc	CFAFr	XOF
Malta	MLT	.mt	M	lira	LM	MTL
Marshall Islands	MHL	.mh	–	US dollar	$, US$	USD
Mauritania	MRT	.mr	RIM	ouguiya	U, UM	MRO
Mauritius	MUS	.mu	MS	rupee	MR, MauRe	MUR
Mexico	MEX	.mx	MEX	peso	Mex$	MXN
Micronesia, Federated States of	FSM	.fm	–	US dollar	$, US$	USD
Moldova	MDA	.md	MD	leu	Mld	MDL
Monaco	MCO	.mc	MC	euro	€	EUR
Mongolia	MNG	.mn	MGL	tugrug	T	MNT
Morocco	MAR	.ma	MA	dirham	DH	MAD
Mozambique	MOZ	.mz	MOC	metical	Mt, MZM	MZM
Myanmar	MMR	.mm	BUR	kyat	K	MMK
Namibia	NAM	.na	NAM	dollar	N$	NAD
Nauru	NRU	.nr	NAU	Australian dollar	A$	AUD
Nepal	NPL	.np	NEP	rupee	NRp, NRs	NPR
The Netherlands	NLD	.nl	NL	euro	€	EUR
New Zealand	NZL	.nz	NZ	dollar	NZ$	NZD
Nicaragua	NIC	.ni	NIC	córdoba	C$	NIO
Niger	NER	.ne	RN	CFA franc	CFAFr	XOF
Nigeria	NGA	.ng	NGR	naira	N	NGN
Norway	NOR	.no	N	krone	NKr	NOK
Oman	OMN	.om	–	rial	RO	OMR
Pakistan	PAK	.pk	PK	rupee	PRs, Rp	PKR
Palau	PLW	.pw	–	US dollar	$, US$	USD

Appendices

Country	ISO country code	Internet suffix	IVR code	Currency	Currency abbreviation	ISO currency code
Panama	PAN	.pa	PA	balboa	B, Ba	PAB
Papua New Guinea	PNG	.pg	PNG	kina	K	PGK
Paraguay	PRY	.py	PY	guaraní	Gs	PYG
Peru	PER	.pe	PE	new sol	Pes	PEN
Philippines	PHL	.ph	RP	peso	PHP	PHP
Poland	POL	.pl	PL	zloty	Zl	PLN
Portugal	PRT	.pt	P	euro	€	EUR
Qatar	QAT	.qa	Q	rial	QR	QAR
Romania	ROU	.ro	RO	leu	L	ROL
Russia	RUS	.ru	RUS	rouble	R	RUB
Rwanda	RWA	.rw	RWA	franc	RF, RWFr	RWF
Samoa	WSM	.ws	WS	tala	ST$	WST
San Marino	SMR	.sm	RSM	euro	€	EUR
São Tomé and Príncipe	STP	.st	–	dobra	Db	STD
Saudi Arabia	SAU	.sa	SA	riyal	SR, SRls	SAR
Senegal	SEN	.sn	SN	CFA franc	CFAFr	XOF
Serbia and Montenegro	YUG	.yu	JCG	dinar/euro	D, Din, €	CSD, EUR
Seychelles	SYC	.sc	SY	rupee	SR	SCR
Sierra Leone	SLE	.sl	WAL	leone	Le	SLL
Singapore	SGP	.sg	SGP	dollar	S$	SGD
Slovakia	SVK	.sk	SK	koruna	Kč	SKK
Slovenia	SVN	.si	SLO	tolar	SIT	SIT
Solomon Islands	SLB	.sb		dollar	SI$	SBD
Somalia	SOM	.so	SO	shilling	SoSh	SOS
South Africa	ZAF	.za	ZA	rand	R	ZAR
Spain	ESP	.es	E	euro	€	EUR
Sri Lanka	LKA	.lk	CL	rupee	SLR, SLRs	LKR
St Kitts and Nevis	KNA	.kn	–	East Caribbean dollar	EC$	XCD

Country	ISO country code	Internet suffix	IVR code	Currency	Currency abbreviation	ISO currency code
St Lucia	LCA	.lc	WL	East Caribbean dollar	EC$	XCD
St Vincent and the Grenadines	VCT	.vc	WV	East Caribbean dollar	EC$	XCD
Sudan	SDN	.sd	SUD	dinar	SD	SDD
Suriname	SUR	.sr	SME	dollar	SRD, $	SRD
Swaziland	SWZ	.sz	SD	lilangeni	Li, E	SZL
Sweden	SWE	.se	S	krona	Skr	SEK
Switzerland	CHE	.ch	CH	franc	SFr, SwF	CHF
Syria	SYR	.sy	SYR	pound	LS, S$	SYP
Taiwan	TWN	.tw	RC	new dollar	NT$	TWD
Tajikistan	TJK	.tj	TJ	somoni	S	TJS
Tanzania	TZA	.tz	EAT	shilling	TSh	TZS
Thailand	THA	.th	T	baht	B	THB
Togo	TGO	.tg	TG	CFA franc	CFAFr	XOF
Tonga	TON	.to	–	pa'anga, dollar	T$	TOP
Trinidad and Tobago	TTO	.tt	TT	dollar	TT$	TTD
Tunisia	TUN	.tn	TN	dinar	TD, D	TND
Turkey	TUR	.tr	TR	lira	TL	TRY
Turkmenistan	TKM	.tm	TM	manat	TMM	TMM
Tuvalu	TUV	.tv	–	Australian dollar	A$	AUD
Uganda	UGA	.ug	EAU	shilling	USh	UGS
Ukraine	UKR	.ua	UA	hryvnia	–	UAH
United Arab Emirates	ARE	.ae	–	dirham	DH	AED
United Kingdom	GBR	.uk	GB	pound sterling	£	GBP
United States of America	USA	.us	USA	dollar	$, US$	USD
Uruguay	URY	.uy	ROU	peso	Ur$, Urug$	UYU

Appendices

Country	ISO country code	Internet suffix	IVR code	Currency	Currency abbreviation	ISO currency code
Uzbekistan	UZB	.uz	UZ	sum	–	UZS
Vanuatu	VUT	.vu	–	vatu	V, VT	VUV
Vatican City	VAT	.va	V	euro	€	EUR
Venezuela	VEN	.ve	YV	bolívar	Bs	VEB
Vietnam	VNM	.vn	VN	dông	D	VND
Yemen	YEM	.ye	YAR	riyal	YR, YRI	YER
Zambia	ZMB	.zm	Z	kwacha	K	ZMK
Zimbabwe	ZWE	.zw	ZW	dollar	Z$	ZWD

Decorations

AC	CGM	DCVO	ISO	MC
AD	CH	DFC	KB	MM
AE	CIE	DFM	KBE	MVO
AFC	CLIT	DSC	KCB	OBE
AFM	CLITT	DSM	KCMG	OC
AK	CMG	DSO	KCVO	OM
AM	CMH	GBE	KG	QPM
AO	CV	GC	KM	QSM
BEM	CVO	GCB	KP	QSO
CB	DBE	GCH	KSTJ	RD
CBE	DCB	GCMG	KT	TD
CDSO	DCM	GCVO	LVO	VC
CG	DCMG	GM	MBE	VMH

Degrees

Bachelors

AB	BARCH	BCOMM	BENG	BLITT
BA	BAS	BD	BESL	BM
BAGR	BCH	BDS	BESS	BMUS
BAGRIC	BCL	BE	BL	BPHARM
BAI	BCOM	BED	BLIT	BPHIL

BRE	BVMANDS	LITB	MB	
BS	CHB	LITTB	MUSB	
BSC	EDB	LLB	SCB	

Diplomas

DA	DIPED	DOMS	HND
DIC	DIPSW	DPH	OND
DIH	DIPTECH	DPM	

Doctors

DC	DENG	DPHIL	LITD	SCD
DCH	DING	DS	LITTD	THD
DCL	DLIT	DSC	LLD	UJD
DD	DLITT	DTH	MD	VMD
DDS	DMUS	JUD	MUSD	
DED	DPH	LHD	PHD	

Licentiates

LCH	LCP	LDS	LRCP	LSA
LCHIR	LCST	LLCM	LRCS	LTH

Masters

AM	LLM	MDS	MPHIL
CHM	MA	MLITT	MSC
CM	MBA	MPHARM	

First Names

Diminutives of some first names are given.

Male

ABE	ANDIE	BAZ	BERT	BOBBY
AL	ANDY	BAZZA	BERTIE	BRAD
ALEC	ARCH	BEN	BILL	BRAM
ALEX	ARCHIE	BENJIE	BILLIE	CHAE
ALF	ARCHY	BENJY	BILLY	CHAS
ALFIE	BART	BENNIE	BOB	CHAY
ALGY	BAT	BERNIE	BOBBIE	CHIC

CHICK	FREDDIE	JOEY	NICHOL	ROD
CHRIS	FREDDY	JON	NICK	RODDY
CHRISTY	GABBY	JOS	NICKY	RUDY
CHUCK	GABI	JOSH	NICOL	SAM
CLEM	GAZ	KEN	NOR	SAMMY
CLINT	GENE	KENNIE	NORM	SANDY
DAI	GEO	KENNY	NYE	SIM
DAN	GEOFF	KEV	OLLIE	TAM
DANNY	GERRIE	KIT	OZZIE	TED
DAVE	GERRY	KURT	OZZY	TEDDIE
DAVIE	GIL	LARRY	PADDY	TEDDY
DAVY	GREG	LAURIE	PAT	TERRY
DEL	GUS	LAWRIE	PERRY	THEO
DEN	GUSSIE	LEN	PET	TIM
DENNY	HAL	LENNIE	PETE	TIMMY
DICK	HANK	LENNY	PHIL	TOM
DICKEN	HERB	LES	PIP	TOMMY
DICKIE	HERBIE	LEW	RAB	TONY
DICKON	HUMPH	LEWIE	RABBIE	VIV
DICKY	IK	LOUIE	RAE	VYV
DOB	IKE	MANNY	RANDY	WALLY
DOBBIN	IKY	MAX	RAY	WATTY
DON	JAKE	MAXIM	REG	WES
DONNIE	JAMIE	MICK	REGGIE	WILL
DREW	JEFF	MICKY	REX	WILLIE
DUD	JEM	MIKE	RICH	WILLS
ED	JERRY	NAT	RICHIE	WILLY
EDDIE	JIM	NATE	RICK	WOODY
EDDY	JIMMY	NED	RICKY	
ERNIE	JO	NEDDIE	ROB	
FRED	JOE	NEDDY	ROBBIE	

Female

ABBY	AILIE	ALLY	BABS	BECCY
ADDIE	ALEX	ANGIE	BARBIE	BECKY
ADDY	ALEXA	ANGY	BEA	BECS
AGGIE	ALI	BAB	BEATTY	BEE
AGGY	ALLIE	BABBIE	BECCA	BEL

BELL	DEBBY	GERRIE	JUD	LOLITA
BELLA	DEBS	GERRY	JUDE	LOU
BELLE	DI	GERT	JUDIE	LOUIE
BESS	DIE	GERTIE	JUDY	LYNN
BESSIE	DO	GILL	JULE	LYNNE
BESSY	DOLLY	GILLY	JULIE	MADGE
BET	DORA	GINA	JULIET	MAG
BETH	DORRIE	GRETA	KATE	MAGDA
BETSY	DOT	GWEN	KATH	MAGGIE
BETTINA	DOTTIE	GWENDA	KATHIE	MAISIE
BETTY	EDIE	GWENNIE	KATHY	MANDY
BEX	EDY	HAN	KATIE	MARGO
BIDDIE	ELIZA	HATTIE	KATY	MAT
BIDDY	ELLA	HATTY	KATYA	MATTY
BREDA	ELLEN	HETTY	KAY	MAUD
BRIDE	ELLIE	IBBY	KIM	MAUDE
BRIDIE	ELMA	ISA	KIRSTIE	MAY
CADDIE	ELSIE	JACKIE	KIRSTY	MEG
CANDY	EM	JACQUI	KIT	MEGAN
CARLIE	EMM	JAN	KITTIE	META
CARLY	ENA	JANEY	KITTY	MILLIE
CARO	ETTA	JANIE	LENA	MINA
CARRIE	ETTIE	JEN	LETTIE	MINNIE
CASS	FANNY	JENNA	LETTY	MO
CASSIE	FLO	JENNIE	LIBBY	MOLL
CATHIE	FLORRIE	JENNY	LINA	MOLLY
CATHY	FLOSSIE	JESS	LINDY	NABBY
CHRIS	FLOY	JESSIE	LISA	NAN
CHRISSIE	FRAN	JESSY	LISBET	NELL
CINDY	FRED	JILL	LISBETH	NELLIE
CIS	FREDA	JINNY	LISE	NELLY
CISSIE	FREDDIE	JO	LISETTE	NETTA
CISSY	FREDDY	JODIE	LIVY	NETTIE
CLEO	GABBY	JOE	LIZ	NICHOL
CON	GABI	JOOLS	LIZA	NICKY
CONNIE	GAIL	JOSIE	LIZBETH	NICOL
DEB	GENE	JOSS	LIZZIE	NITA
DEBBIE	GEORGIE	JOZY	LOLA	NORA

Appendices

NORAH	PRUE	STACEY	TESSA	TRIX
PADDY	RACH	STACY	THEO	TRIXIE
PAM	RAE	STEPH	TIB	TRUDY
PAMMY	RAY	SUE	TIBBIE	VAL
PAT	RENE	SUKE	TIBBY	VI
PATSY	RITA	SUKIE	TILDA	VIC
PATTY	ROS	SUKY	TILLY	VICKIE
PEG	ROZ	SUS	TINA	VICKY
PEGGY	SADIE	SUSIE	TORI	VIV
PEN	SAL	SUSY	TORY	VYV
PENNY	SALLY	SUZY	TRACY	WIN
PIPPA	SANDRA	TEENIE	TRICIA	WINNIE
POLL	SANDY	TERRY	TRISH	
POLLY	SINDY	TESS	TRISHA	

Roman Numerals

1	I		20	XX
2	II		30	XXX
3	III		40	XL
4	IV		50	L
5	V		60	LX
6	VI		70	LXX
7	VII		80	LXXX
8	VIII		90	XC
9	IX		100	C
10	X		200	CC
11	XI		300	CCC
12	XII		400	CD
13	XIII		500	D
14	XIV		600	DC
15	XV		700	DCC
16	XVI		800	DCCC
17	XVII		900	CM
18	XVIII		1,000	M
19	XIX		2,000	MM

Medieval Roman Numerals

7	S		2,000	Z
11	O		3,000	B
40	F		5,000	A
50	A		11,000	O
70	S		40,000	F
80	R		70,000	S
90	N		80,000	R
150	Y		90,000	N
160	T		150,000	Y
200	H		160,000	T
250	E, K		200,000	H
300	B		250,000	E
400	G, P		400,000	G, P
500	A, Q			

Serviceman, Servicewoman

Solvers may need to check which gender is appropriate for a particular clue.

AAQMG	BRIGGEN	COS	LOOT	QMS
AB	CAPT	CPL	LT	RA
AC	CDR	CPO	LTCDR	RSM
ACM	CDRE	CSM	LTCOL	SERG
ACW	CG	DAAG	LTGEN	SERGT
ADJ	CGS	DAG	MAJ	SGT
ADJT	CIC	DL	NCO	SM
ADM	CIGS	DOC	OC	SO
AF	CINC	FM	OD	SPR
AG	CMDR	FO	OPS	SQNLDR
AOC	CO	GI	OS	VA
AR	COFS	GOC	PFC	WCDR
ATS	COM	GSO	PO	WO
AVM	COMDR	LAC	PTE	
BC	COMDT	LACW	PVT	
BDR	COMM	LCPL	QM	
BRIG	CORP	LIEUT	QMG	

Appendices

Unions

The list includes trade unions, political groups, sports associations, countries and other organisations of various kinds.

ACLU	EBU	IUPAC	PCS	UNIFI
AEEU	ECU	KANU	RFU	UNITA
AU	EGU	LGU	RMT	UOM
BECTU	EMU	MSF	TANDG	UPU
BIFU	ESU	NASUWT	TGWU	USDAW
CCCP	EU	NFU	TU	USSR
CDU	EUW	NUJ	UCAR	WEU
CGT	FBU	NUM	UCATT	ZANU
CSEU	GMB	NUS	UCI	ZAPU
CU	GPMU	NUT	UDM	
CWU	ITU	OILC	UEFA	

US States

State Abbreviation

Only those states which use an abbreviation of the state name are included.

AK	HI	MI	NV	UT
AL	IA	MN	NY	VA
AR	ID	MO	OH	VT
AZ	IL	MS	OK	WA
CA	IN	MT	OR	WI
CO	KS	NC	PA	WV
CT	KY	ND	RI	WY
DC	LA	NE	SC	
DE	MA	NH	SD	
FL	MD	NJ	TN	
GA	ME	NM	TX	

Zip Code

ALA	KY	NEV	VA
ARIZ	LA	NH	VT
ARK	MASS	NJ	WASH
CALIF	MD	NMEX	WIS
COLO	ME	NY	WVA
CONN	MICH	OKLA	WYO
DC	MINN	OREG	
DEL	MISS	PA	
FLA	MO	RI	
GA	MONT	SC	
ILL	NC	SDAK	
IND	NDAK	TENN	
KANS	NEBR	TEX